PINES PICKS:
A Teen's Guide to the
Best Things to Eat and
Drink in New York City

By David D. Pines

teenage foodie

Pines Picks

A Teen's Guide to the Best Things to Eat and Drink in New York City

Third Edition

By David D. Pines

Conifer Press

Published by Conifer Press, Austin, Texas
Copyright ©2016 David D. Pines
All rights reserved.

Index: Elena Gwynn, www.QuillAndInkIndexing.com

Cover and Interior design: Bella Guzmán, www.highwirecreative.com

Interior layout: Davis Creative, www.DavisCreative.com

Cover copy: Jenny Magic, www.betterwaytosayit.com

Library of Congress Control Number: 2011945149

ISBN: 978-0-9847108-3-6

Quantity discounts are available on bulk purchases of this book for educational, gift purposes, or as premiums for increasing magazine subscriptions or renewals. Special books or book excerpts can also be created to fit specific needs. For information, please contact info@pinespicks.com or 512-250-8546

TABLE OF CONTENTS

PREFACE

It has been about two years since the last edition of *Pines Picks* was published. Now that I am a little older, I have been able to get around to try more foods and places both inside and outside of NYC. Once again, several of my favorite NYC restaurants — places I really loved that had standout dishes — closed their doors during that short time. I am sad to report this list of Restaurants in Peace™ ("RIP") establishments, which includes as of this printing:

RIP

Black Hound

BLT Burger

Brasserie

David Burke Townhouse

Pommes Frites

Rockaway Taco

Ronnybrook Milk Bar

This Little Piggy Had Roast Beef

I will miss them.

But, the great thing about the dining scene in NYC is that there are always new places to try. So I again set out to track the newcomers and to try places I had not visited before, as well as to make sure my previous picks were still accurate. I had even more fun doing this new round of "food hunts," and continue to believe that NYC is the best place to eat in the whole world.

The result is the Third Edition of *Pines Picks*. Happy Eating!

INTRODUCTION

I am now a tenth grader in New York City, which is unquestionably one of the best places in the whole world to eat and to try all different types of foods. Restaurants are a big part of our lives here; we go out to eat or order in a lot. And believe me, there are so many places to try, it can make your head spin! In writing this book, I set out to find the most amazing foods in the city, describe them for you, and tell you where to try them. With the help of family and friends, I went on "food hunts" all over New York City to find the best dishes. These "hunts" were tremendously fun (and really filling!), and were the foundation of my research. I'm very excited to share the results with you.

A couple of notes about this book: I always provide my pick for the winner, which I call the "Pines Pick." When I like another restaurant almost as much, it is listed as a runner up. Since this is a kid and teen-friendly book, I did not mention places that were unfriendly or unwelcoming to kids or teens. While I did a lot of research and brainstorming with others to find the best dishes, keep in mind that there are thousands of restaurants in NYC, and the restaurant scene is constantly changing. That is why I am always open to and grateful for new ideas. So please let me know if you feel strongly about other places, and I will try them for possible inclusion in future updates. I am particularly interested in hearing about great foods outside of Manhattan, since I still know that part of the city best. You can contact me through my website at www.pinespicks.com or send me an email at suggestions@pinespicks.com.

David Pines

CHAPTER **1**

BREAKFAST FOODS

BAGELS

The Bagel Store
www.thebagelstoreonline.com

754 Metropolitan Avenue
(between Humboldt Street & Graham Avenue)
Brooklyn, NY 11211
(646) 883-1467

349 Bedford Avenue
(between 3rd & 4th Streets)
Brooklyn, NY 11211
(929) 336-3264

The Bagel Store probably has the best variety of bagels in the world. From the Rainbow Bagel to the Bacon, Egg and Cheese Bagel, the Bagel Store has added some incredible creativity to the world of bagels. My favorite bagel is the unique Rainbow Bagel which couldn't be further from the usual brownish color with its vibrant rainbow color throughout. I love the sweet tasting glaze on the Rainbow Bagel, which really makes the bagel glisten. With the addition of a pinch of salt, and the smooth texture of the bagel, it is my favorite in NYC. Also, I really think the cinnamon sugar bagel is delicious due to its super soft roll-like texture. It really melts in your mouth and has the perfect flavor. Overall, the Bagel Store is a unique place serving up some outstanding, must-try bagels.

RUNNER UP

Bagel Hole

www.bagelhole.net

400 Seventh Avenue
(between Twelveth & 13th Avenues)
Brooklyn, NY 11215
(718) 788-4014

RUNNER UP

H&H Midtown Bagels

www.hhmidtownbagels.com

1551 Second Avenue
(between 80th & 81st Streets)
New York, NY 10028
(212) 734-7441

BREAKFAST DUMPLINGS

Norma's
www.normasnyc.com

119 West 56th Street
(between Sixth and Seventh Avenues)
New York, NY 10019
(212) 708-7460

Norma's is the first place I had ever seen that serves breakfast dumplings, so I got extremely excited about trying them. Though I was hoping for the best, I was a little afraid each dumpling might turn out to be a disastrously heavy mini-omelet with clumpy pieces of food in it that the chef called a "breakfast dumpling" just to be different. But, what arrived at the table was exactly what I was hoping for – light, airy, small, fragrant, delicious dumplings. The breakfast dumplings come out steaming, and are filled with fluffy scrambled eggs and finely chopped mushrooms and shrimp. They are served with a sweet and sour sesame sauce, which matches perfectly with the dumplings. It is worth going to Norma's just to try the dumplings! The dumplings are undoubtedly a unique standout dish.

BREAKFAST SANDWICH

BEC
www.becnyc.com

148 Eighth Avenue
(between 17th & 18th Streets)
New York, NY 10011
(212) 633-8020

Served on a nice, soft cheese roll, the Bacon, Egg and Cheese Sandwich from BEC is my favorite breakfast sandwich in NYC. It has melted cheese, and is served with a skinny, over-easy egg, some salt and pepper and thick-cut, perfectly cooked bacon. The bacon is really delicious and pleasantly salty, while the egg has a runny center offsetting the saltiness. A sensational sandwich!

Sarabeth's Kitchen
www.sarabeth.com

1295 Madison Avenue
(at 92nd Street)
New York, NY 10128
(212) 410-7335

339 Greenwich Street
(between Harrison & Jay Streets)
New York, NY 10013
(212) 966-0421

381 Park Avenue South
(between 26th & 27th Streets)
New York, NY 10016

40 Central Park South
(between Fifth & Sixth Avenues)
New York, NY 10019
(212) 826-5959

423 Amsterdam Avenue
(between 80th & 81st Streets)
New York, NY 10024
(212) 496-6280

424 Fifth Avenue
(between 38th & 39th Streets)
Lord & Taylor – 5th Floor
New York, NY 10018
(212) 966-0421

75 Ninth Avenue
(between 15th & 16th Streets)
New York, NY 10011
(212) 989-2424

Sarabeth's Kitchen has my favorite egg dish in the world, called "Goldie Lox." It consists of scrambled eggs, smoked salmon, and cream cheese (I love it with egg whites). It even comes with your choice of muffin – I recommend the toasted English muffin, which is super thick and not anything like the ones you buy in the supermarket. The eggs and toasted English muffin go nicely with jelly on top of them. Sarabeth's Kitchen has good, high-quality jelly, but some flavors are better than others. They switch off sometimes so it may be hard to get the best one: strawberry raspberry. When it is available, be sure to try it. If you want, you can pile the eggs onto the muffin and make yourself a "Goldie Lox" sandwich. It's a delicious breakfast, and definitely a great way to start the day. The cool thing about Sarabeth's Kitchen is that they have so many food combinations you do not expect to work, but they all end up being delicious.

Runner Up listings continued on the next page...

EGGS

RUNNER UP

Bubby's

www.bubbys.com

120 Hudson Street
(at North Moore Street)
New York, NY 10013
(212) 219-0666

71 Gansevoort Street
(at Washington Street)
New York, NY 10014
(212) 206-6200

RUNNER UP

EJ's Luncheonette

www.ejsluncheonette.com

1271 Third Avenue
(at 73rd Street)
New York, NY 10021
(212) 472-0600

Redeye Grill

www.redeyegrill.com

890 Seventh Avenue
(at 56th Street)
New York, NY 10019
(212) 541-9000

Here's a confession: Eggs Benedict is my favorite breakfast dish. It is not the healthiest dish, but I have tried it at many places. Redeye Grill serves it on three perfectly toasted bruschetta bread pieces. The eggs are skillfully poached, and when your spoon sinks in to the egg, the gooey, drippy yolk comes sailing out. Then, there is a fresh Hollandaise sauce that is creamy and a bright yellowish-orange color. When you mix all the flavors together, you get this crazy delicious taste that I cannot wait to experience again. If you like Eggs Benedict, you will love them at Redeye Grill, which is a super kid-friendly place with big metal sculptures of giant dancing shrimp. It's a fun place with good food.

RUNNER UP

Isabella's

www.isabellas.com

359 Columbus Avenue
(at 77th Street)
New York, NY 10024
(212) 724-2100

RUNNER UP

The Mark Restaurant

www.themarkrestaurantnyc.com

25 East 77th Street
(between Fifth & Madison Avenues)
New York, NY 10075
(212) 606-3030

Runner Up listings continued on the next page...

EGGS BENEDICT

Sarabeth's Kitchen

www.sarabeth.com

1295 Madison Avenue
(at 92nd Street)
New York, NY 10128
(212) 410-7335

339 Greenwich Street
(between Harrison & Jay Streets)
New York, NY 10013
(212) 966-0421

381 Park Avenue South
(between 26th & 27th Streets)
New York, NY 10016

40 Central Park South
(between Fifth & Sixth Avenues)
New York, NY 10019
(212) 826-5959

423 Amsterdam Avenue
(between 80th & 81st Streets)
New York, NY 10024
(212) 496-6280

424 Fifth Avenue
(between 38th & 39th Streets)
Lord & Taylor – 5th Floor
New York, NY 10018
(212) 966-0421

75 Ninth Avenue
(between 15th & 16th Streets)
New York, NY 10011
(212) 989-2424

FRENCH TOAST

Norma's
www.normasnyc.com

119 West 56th Street
(between Sixth & Seventh Avenues)
New York, NY 10019
(212) 708-7460

The French Toast at Norma's is super chocolaty. It actually tastes like chocolate cake, and is even covered with chocolate sauce. At about half a foot high, it is the monster of French toast, and I can barely eat three quarters of it. It has a rich chocolate flavor, but is so light it will amaze you. Although you can see the crust of the bread, it is so soaked, you cannot feel the texture of the crust – which is a good thing in my book. Topped with fresh strawberries and pistachios, this stuff is crazy GOOD!

PANCAKES

Pink Tea Cup

www.thepinkteacuprestaurant.com

120 Lafayette Avenue
(between Carlton Avenue & Cumberland Street)
Brooklyn, NY 11238
(347) 227-7472

Pink Tea Cup is a cool chicken and waffle restaurant with great breakfast foods. The pancakes are big, but light and fluffy to the extreme. They come in regular or sweet potato, both of which are excellent. The sweet potato pancakes are sweet, but not overwhelmingly so. All of the pancakes here are topped with powdered sugar. If you try Pink Tea Cup's pancakes, you won't forget them.

RUNNER UP

EJ's Luncheonette

www.ejsluncheonette.com

1271 Third Avenue
(at 73rd Street)
New York, NY 10021
(212) 472-0600

RUNNER UP

Good Enough to Eat

www.goodenoughtoeat.com

520 Columbus Avenue
(at 85th Street)
New York, NY 10024
(212) 496-0163

SAUSAGE

Sarabeth's Kitchen

www.sarabeth.com

1295 Madison Avenue
(at 92nd Street)
New York, NY 10128
(212) 410-7335

339 Greenwich Street
(between Harrison & Jay Streets)
New York, NY 10013
(212) 966-0421

381 Park Avenue South
(between 26th & 27th Streets)
New York, NY 10016

40 Central Park South
(between Fifth & Sixth Avenues)
New York, NY 10019
(212) 826-5959

423 Amsterdam Avenue
(between 80th & 81st Streets)
New York, NY 10024
(212) 496-6280

424 Fifth Avenue
(between 38th & 39th Streets)
Lord & Taylor – 5th Floor
New York, NY 10018
(212) 966-0421

75 Ninth Avenue
(between 15th & 16th Streets)
New York, NY 10011
(212) 989-2424

Every time I eat breakfast at Sarabeth's Kitchen, I can't help but place a side order for the chicken apple sausage. Thick, savory, sweet, and cooked just right, the chicken apple sausage is served with a side of Sarabeth's fresh apricot preserves. Not sure how they do it, but it's the best chicken apple sausage around, and it really adds to the meal. Order some for the table and before you know it everyone will be digging in and cutting off little pieces for themselves.

WAFFLES

Wafels and Dinges

www.wafelsanddinges.com

Check the website for the weekly truck schedule but for the most up-to-date info, call the Hot Wafeline at **866-429-7329** or check Twitter (**@waffletruck**).

Wafels and Dinges is actually a mobile restaurant in a truck. There is a website that will help you locate their trucks. As far as I am concerned, these waffles are by far the best in the city and are still unbeatable. They come perfectly cooked with a sweet glaze on them and have a nice, sugary taste. I like to order my waffles with Belgian chocolate and ice cream, but all the varieties are great. Also, the "de throwdown wafel" with spekuloos spread and whipped cream is gingerbread heaven. These chewy, hot, fresh waffles are so amazing; you are unlikely to have tasted anything like them before.

RUNNER UP
Amy Ruth's

www.amyruthsharlem.com

113 West 116th Street
(between Lennox & Seventh Avenues)
New York, NY 10026
(212) 280-8779

RUNNER UP
Petite Abeille

www.petiteabeille.com

401 East 20th Street
(at First Avenue)
New York, NY 10010
(212) 727-1505

44 West 17th Street
(between Fifth & Sixth Avenues)
New York, NY 10011
(212) 727-2989

CHAPTER **2**

LUNCH AND DINNER FOODS

BUFFALO WINGS

Rare Bar and Grill

www.rarebarandgrill.com

152 West 26th Street
(between Sixth & Seventh Avenue)
New York, NY 10001
(212) 807-7273

303 Lexington Avenue
(between East 37th & 38th Streets)
New York, NY 10016
(212) 481-1999

I have tried many wings and wings are one of my favorite foods, but after finding the "lollipop wings" at Rare Bar and Grill, my standards for Buffalo wings have changed forever. The wings at Rare are perfect in all aspects. From heat to messiness to crispiness to the importance of a solid blue cheese dip, these wings are flawless. They have a nice medium to spicy heat and a traditional buffalo flavored sauce and are easily accessible without having to get super messy due to the bone sticking up, hence earning the name of "lollipop wings." I really think they nailed the crispiness factor — supplying the perfect crispy skin without taking away the moist interior. And lastly, the warm Roquefort fondue that comes with the wings has perfectly tangy-sweet tastiness and supplies the essential cooling of a good blue cheese dip. All in all, the best wings I have had in my life.

Blondies Sports

www.blondiessports.com

212 West 79th Street
(between Amsterdam Avenue & Broadway)
New York, NY 10024
(212) 362-4360

Runner Up listings continued on the next page...

BUFFALO WINGS

Atomic Wings

www.atomicwings.com

@ The Blue Room
1140 Second Avenue
(at 60th Street)
New York, NY 10065
(212) 888-5777

@ Bar Coastal
1495 First Avenue
(at 78th Street)
New York, NY 10021
(212) 772-8400

@ Down the Hatch
179 West 4th Street
(between Sixth & Seventh Avenues)
New York, NY 10014
(212) 627-9500

184 First Avenue
(between 11th & 12th Streets)
New York, NY 10009
(212) 505-7272

2090 Frederick Douglass Boulevard
(at 113th Street)
New York, NY 10026
(212) 666-2904

311 Broadway
(between Duane & Thomas Streets)
New York, NY 10007
(212) 571-7667

528 Ninth Avenue
(between 39th & 40th Streets)
New York, NY 10018
(212) 760-9090

160 West 25th Street
(between Sixth & Seventh Avenue)
New York, NY 10001
(212) 337-8301

1830 Second Avenue
(between 94th & 95th Streets)
New York, NY 10128
(212) 410-3800

BURGER

The Polo Bar

http://www.ralphlauren.com/shop/index.jsp?categoryId=54938256

1 East 55th Street
New York, NY 10022
(212) 207-8562

Ralph Lauren's restaurant in New York City is a very challenging reservation to get. After multiple tries, I finally reserved a table at this club-like restaurant. A bouncer-like man stands at the entrance with a list, only allowing people with reservations to enter. I had heard great things about the restaurant, and was super excited to try all the food. But, one dish stood out from all the rest. This impeccably refined dish was "The Polo Burger." The perfect bacon cheeseburger arrives with a cone of French fries, a silver bucket of ketchup, and a deli pickle. The burger is picture perfect — from the large fluffy sesame seed bun to clean, crisp whitish-green lettuce to the super thinly sliced pickles, tomato and red onions to the thin square of cheddar cheese and the deep red chewy, yet crunchy bacon. But, in the end, the taste of this burger outdoes its good looks and the juiciness of the soft medium-cooked meat is the real star. Accompanied by the saltiness of the bacon and the refreshing veggies, with the addition of a little ketchup, the blend of all of the ingredients creates one incredibly good, special-occasion burger.

Burger Joint

www.burgerjointny.com

Le Parker Meridien
119 West 56th Street
(between Sixth & Seventh Avenues)
New York, NY 10019
(212) 708-7414

33 West 8th Street
(between Fifth Avenue & MacDougal Street)
New York, NY 10011
(212) 432-1400

Runner Up listings continued on next page...

BURGER

Shake Shack

www.shakeshack.com

154 East 86th Street
(between Lexington & Third Avenue)
New York, NY 10128
(646) 237-5035

215 Murray Street
(between North End Avenue & West Street)
New York, NY 10282
(646) 545-4600

366 Columbus Avenue
(at 77th Street)
New York, NY 10024
(646) 747-8770

691 Eighth Avenue
(at 44th Street)
New York, NY 10036
(646) 435-0135

Citi Field
12301 Roosevelt Avenue
(behind the scoreboard)
Flushing (Queens), NY 11368

Madison Square Park
(Near Madison Avenue & East 23rd Street)
New York, NY 10010
(212) 889-6600

600 Third Avenue
(at East 40th Street)
New York, NY 10016
(646) 668-4880

49 Grand Central Terminal
(Lower Level Dining Concourse)
New York, NY 10017
(646) 517-5805

BurgerFi

www.burgerfi.com

1571 Second Avenue
(between 81st & 82nd Streets)
New York, NY 10028
(646) 684-3172

CHEESESTEAKS

Carl's Steaks

www.carlssteaks.com

1 East 161st Street
(Yankee Stadium)
Bronx, NY 10451

Carl's steaks and 99 Miles to Philly are hands down my two favorite restaurants for cheesesteaks in NYC. It is a really difficult decision, but I currently like Carl's Steaks the best. My dad went to school in Philadelphia, and has taken me there many times to eat the cheesesteaks he loved when he was a student. The steaks at Carl's are really authentic. The great hoagie roll and the chopped sirloin steak make for a very flavorful and hearty sandwich. Served hot with some "cheese whiz" and sweet grilled onions, it is truly an amazing treat.

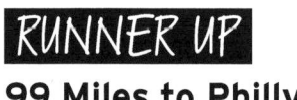

99 Miles to Philly

94 Third Avenue
(between 12th & 13th Streets)
New York, NY 10003
(212) 253-2700

CHICKEN FINGERS/TENDERS

Sticky's Finger Joint
www.stickys.com

31 West Eighth Street
(between Fifth Avenue & MacDougal Street)
New York, NY 10011
(212) 777-7131

484 Third Avenue
(between 32nd & 33rd Streets)
New York, NY 10016

Your view of chicken fingers will never be the same after trying the different types of fingers loaded with toppings at Sticky's Finger Joint. The folks at Sticky's take perfectly fried chicken fingers and add a variety of sauces and toppings to create some interesting combinations that are simply delicious. My favorites are the General Sticky Tso, the Honey BBQ Club, and the Salted Caramel Pretzel. All three types contain an explosion of flavors. The General Sticky Tso has a nice sweet and spicy mixture. The Honey BBQ has a delicious sauce that is sweet and tangy with some cheddar cheese and bacon bits. And, the Salted Caramel Pretzel dessert is unlike any chicken tender I have ever had previously: it contains an addictive caramel sauce with perfect saltiness. The batter on all of the tenders is very thin and all of the tender dishes are creative and tasty! If you like chicken fingers and are ready to experiment with some new flavors, I highly recommend Sticky's.

Popeyes

www.popeyes.com

Numerous locations throughout NYC

FRENCH FRIES

The Grey Dog
www.thegreydog.com

242 West 16th Street
(between Seventh & Eighth Avenues)
New York, NY 10011
(212) 229-2345

244 Mulberry Street
(between Spring & Prince Streets)
New York, NY 10012
(212) 966-1060

49 Carmine Street
(between Bedford & Bleecker Streets)
New York, NY 10014
(212) 462-0041

The thin, crispy, beautifully-golden fries at The Grey Dog are served in a paper bag and are just amazing. They are not too oily and have the right amount of salt on them. With the addition of some ketchup, these fries are ideal and sure to satisfy any craving for top-notch fries.

FRIED CHICKEN

Blue Ribbon Fried Chicken

www.blueribbonfriedchicken.com

28 East 1st Street
(between Extra Place & 2nd Street)
New York, NY 10003
(212) 228-0404

The key to the fried chicken at Blue Ribbon is the spices. The perfectly spiced, super flavorful fried chicken is one-of-a-kind. The many spices give the chicken an incredible flavor: it is deliciously spicy without going overboard. The skin on the fried chicken is also a highlight. It is thin and crisp, yet it still keeps the chicken moist. I especially love the drumsticks. You can enjoy the fried chicken with a bunch of cool sauces; my favorite sauce is the sweet clover honey which adds a layer of delectable sweetness.

RUNNER UP

The Dutch

www.thedutchnyc.com

131 Sullivan Street
(at Prince Street)
New York, NY 10012
212-677-6200

GRILLED CHEESE

Murray's Cheese Shop
www.murrayscheese.com

254 Bleeker Street
(between Sixth & Seventh Avenue)
New York, NY 10014
(212) 243-3289

I have tried a lot of grilled cheese sandwiches. Many are hard to remember. However, the grilled cheese at Murray's Cheese Shop really stood out to me. I got "The Murray's Melt," which contains a mixture of tasty cheeses on super crispy bread. The bread is a golden brown color and supplies an unmatchable crunch. The grilled cheese was so gooey that a lot of melted cheese rolled out after I took the first bite. I really enjoy the flavor in the mixture of cheeses that is used at Murray's as well as the buttery flavor in the bread.

Little Muenster
www.littlemuenster.com

225 Liberty Street
(Hudson Eats at Brookfield Place)
New York, NY 10002
(212) 786-0186

RUNNER UP

The Melt Shop
www.meltshop.com

55 West 26th Street
(between Broadway and Sixth Avenue)
New York, NY 10010
(212) 447-6358

Runner Up listings continued on next page...

GRILLED CHEESE

'Wichcraft

www.wichcraftnyc.com

1 Rockefeller Plaza
(at 49th Street between Fifth & Sixth
Avenues)
New York, NY 10020
(212) 780-0577

11 East 20th Street
(between Broadway & Fifth Avenue)
New York, NY 10003

397 Greenwich Street
(at Beach Street)
New York, NY 10013
(212) 780-0577

440 East 29th Street
(at East River)
New York, NY 10016
(212) 780-0577

555 Fifth Avenue
(at 46th Street)
New York, NY 10017
(212) 780-0577

60 East 8th Street
(at Mercer Street)
New York, NY 10003
(212) 780-0577

601 West 26th Street
(between Eleventh & Twelfth Avenues)
New York, NY 10001
(212) 780-0577

61 West 62nd Street
(between Broadway & Columbus Avenue)
New York, NY 10023
(212) 780-0577

HOT DOG

Bark Hot Dogs
www.barkhotdogs.com

474 Bergen Street
(between Fifth & Flatbush Avenues)
Brooklyn, NY 11217
(718) 789-1939

The hot dogs at Bark Hot Dogs are awesome. They are not strongly flavored, and are not overly juicy or burnt. The buns are toasted with a slight buttery taste, and when you take a bite, all the flavors really come together well. I tried several varieties of Bark dogs with different toppings, and particularly enjoyed the tangy sauerkraut and flavorful mustard. The relish and pickles are also very good and add nice flavor to the dogs. There are lots of other toppings to choose from including chili and raw red onions. All in all, you can't go wrong with a Bark dog.

RUNNER UP

Crif Dogs

www.crifdogs.com

113 Saint Marks Place
(between Avenue A & First Avenue)
New York, NY 10009
(212) 614-2728

555 Driggs Avenue
(between 6th & 7th Streets)
Brooklyn, NY 11211
(718) 302-3200

RUNNER UP

Katz's

www.katzsdelicatessen.com

205 East Houston Street
(at Ludlow Street)
New York, NY 10002
(212) 254-2246

Runner Up listings continued on next page...

HOT DOG

Shake Shack

www.shakeshack.com

154 East 86th Street
(between Lexington & Third Avenues)
New York, NY 10128
(646) 237-5035

215 Murray Street
(between North End Avenue & West Street)
New York, NY 10282
(646) 545-4600

366 Columbus Avenue
(at 77th Street)
New York, NY 10024
(646) 747-8770

691 Eighth Avenue
(at 44th Street)
New York, NY 10036
(646) 435-0135

Citi Field
12301 Roosevelt Avenue
(behind the scoreboard)
Flushing (Queens), NY 11368

Madison Square Park
(Near Madison Avenue & East 23rd Street)
New York, NY 10010
(212) 889-6600

600 Third Avenue
(at East 40th Street)
New York, NY 10016
(646) 668-4880

49 Grand Central Terminal
(Lower Level Dining Concourse)
New York, NY 10017
(646) 517-5805

MACARONI AND CHEESE

S'MAC
www.smacnyc.com

345 East 12th Street
(between First & Second Avenues)
New York, NY 10003
(212) 358-7912

S'MAC has an incredible variety of macaroni and cheese dishes, which come in four sizes from a snack to a giant party platter. I tried the classic four cheese variety and the Buffalo chicken mac and cheese. Both were delicious and hot with a delectable crispy top. But, the Buffalo chicken mac and cheese is something really special, especially since I love the taste of Buffalo wings. The Buffalo mac is spicy and very cheesy with some definite blue cheese flavor — all in all, a very cool and unique dish. Thinking about the macaroni and cheese dishes at S'MAC actually makes my mouth water.

RUNNER UP

Brother Jimmy's BBQ

www.brotherjimmys.com

1 East 161st Street
(at Yankee Stadium)
Bronx, NY 10451

116 East 16th Street
(between Park Avenue South & Irving Place)
New York, NY 10003
(212) 673-6465

1485 Second Avenue
(between 77th & 78th Streets)
New York, NY 10075
(212) 288-0999

181 Lexington Avenue
(between 31st & 32nd Streets)
New York, NY 10016
(212) 779-7427

416 Eighth Avenue
(at 31st Street)
New York, NY 10001
(212) 967-7603

Runner Up listings continued on next page...

MACARONI AND CHEESE

MacBar

www.macbar.net

54 Prince Street
(between Mulberry & Lafayette Streets)
New York, NY 10012
(212) 226-0211

Max Brenner

www.maxbrenner.com

841 Broadway
(between 13th & 14th Streets)
New York, NY 10003
(212) 388-0030

MOZZARELLA STICKS

Pluck U
www.plucku.us

230 Thompson Street
(between West Third & Bleecker Streets)
New York, NY 10012
(212) 979-2468

I wouldn't have guessed it either, but the mozzarella sticks at Pluck U are the best I've had. They easily qualify as amazing. Made to order, they are cooked to perfection. I am actually able to pull each stick apart as wide as my arms can go and watch the gooey, hot cheese spread all the way across! The sticks themselves aren't too fat and have a flavorful breading that is the perfect balance to the smooth, mild cheese. The sticks come with a well-spiced tomato sauce for dipping. All in all, it is a fantastic mozzarella stick experience.

ONION RINGS

BurgerFi
www.burgerfi.com

1571 Second Avenue
(between 81st & 82nd Streets)
New York, NY 10028
(646) 684-3172

The onion rings at BurgerFi are gigantic! The onion inside the batter comes in one piece, not tiny chopped bits, and is juicy. It is a delicious, sweet onion inside a crispy, thin batter. Each bite is fluffy with a thin air pocket between the batter and the onion adding a complexity to the rings that is unbelievably good.

RUNNER UP

Lucky's Famous Burgers

www.luckysfamousburgers.com

147 East Houston Street
(between Forsyth & Eldridge Streets)
New York, NY 10002
(212) 254-4900

264 West 23rd Street
(between Seventh & Eighth Avenues)
New York, NY 10019
(212) 242-4900

370 West 52nd Street
(between Eighth & Ninth Avenues)
New York, NY 10011
(212) 247-6717

PASTA - BAKED ZITI

Arturo's
www.arturoscafe.com

1617 York Avenue
(at 85th Street)
New York, NY 10028
(212) 535-4480

Few make good baked ziti, but very few make great baked ziti. Over the course of the past two years, I have enjoyed the baked ziti from Arturo's even more than I did before. They make great baked ziti, with a lot of melted cheese. And, it is cooked in an amazing fresh sauce. Arturo's is a favorite neighborhood pizza place – my brother found it when he was nearby. It was a really good discovery, especially if you are up for some excellent baked ziti.

PASTA - CAPELLINI

Il Postino
www.ilpostinony.com

337 East 49th Street
(between First & Second Avenues)
New York, NY 10017
(212) 688-0033

Il Postino is a fancy restaurant (more of a special occasion restaurant than an everyday place due to its high prices), but every once in a while my parents take me and my brother there for dinner. The staff has always been super nice to us, and each time I go there I am amazed at how good the pasta tastes – especially the extremely thin capellini (like angel hair) pasta. Cooked slightly al dente, the capellini is amazingly good, especially with fresh tomato sauce. I like mine a little spicy, and they will adjust it to your liking. Il Postino is an excellent restaurant, and there is just something special about this dish that I really enjoy.

PASTA - PLAIN ZITI AND SAUCE

Don Giovanni Ristorante

www.dongiovanni-ny.com

214 Tenth Avenue
(between 22nd & 23rd Streets)
New York, NY 10011
(212) 242-9054

358 West 44th Street
(between Eighth & Ninth Avenues)
New York, NY 10036
(212) 581-4939

Don Giovanni is a nice family place, and a fun place to go with a group for really good pasta and pizza. For some reason, I love the plain ziti with fresh tomato sauce at Don Giovanni. It's a really simple dish, which tastes great. The portions at Don Giovanni are large and the food is delicious. It makes me hungry just thinking about it.

PASTA - SPAGHETTI AND MEATBALLS

Patsy's Italian Restaurant

www.patsys.com

236 West 56th Street
(between Broadway & Eighth Avenue)
New York, NY 10019
(212) 247-3491

For classic spaghetti and meatballs and cool decorations featuring celebrity pics, you just can't beat Patsy's. The meatballs are delicious and arrive perfectly cooked on a pile of thin, al dente spaghetti. The dish is topped with hot bubbling tomato sauce, which is savory and not too sweet, with the right spices.

(Note: This is Patsy's Italian Restaurant – not to be confused with Patsy's Pizzeria restaurants, which also serve pasta dishes.)

PASTRAMI SANDWICH

Pastrami Queen
www.pastramiqueen.com

1125 Lexington Avenue
(between 78th & 79th Streets)
New York, NY 10075
(212) 734-1500

Sure NYC is known for its delicatessens – there are many excellent ones. But in my book, if you are looking for the best pastrami sandwich in NYC, go straight to Pastrami Queen. I always order mine extra lean. The pastrami is thinly sliced and piled high on good, chewy rye bread. It is lean and flavorful, and frankly just amazing. Served with some spicy deli mustard and half-sour pickles, no pastrami sandwich could be better.

RUNNER UP
Carnegie Deli

www.carnegiedeli.com

854 Seventh Avenue
(at 55th Street)
New York, NY 10019
(212) 757-2245

RUNNER UP
Katz's

www.katzsdelicatessen.com

(Note: if you like fattier, much more thickly sliced pastrami, you will want to check out Katz's Delicatessen, which many people like and I have also grown to appreciate.)

205 East Houston Street
(at Ludlow Street)
New York, NY 10002
(212) 254-2246

PEANUT BUTTER AND
JELLY SANDWICH

Peanut Butter & Co.
www.ilovepeanutbutter.com

240 Sullivan Street
(between West 3rd & Bleecker Streets)
New York, NY 10012
(212) 677-3995

I love this place. They have many different flavored peanut butters as well as regular ones. My favorite is White Chocolate Wonderful. They have excellent peanut butter ice cream sundaes and sandwiches named after famous peanut butter lovers like the Elvis (which is a peanut butter, bacon, and banana sandwich). I ordered the classic on white bread, and it was everything I had hoped for. They let me pick my jelly flavor from a selection of strawberry, grape, and apricot. I also got to pick whether I wanted smooth, chunky or flavored peanut butter, and whether I wanted my sandwich on white or wheat. In the end, I ordered smooth peanut butter with strawberry jelly on white bread: it was creamy and delicious. There is simply no better place to have a peanut butter sandwich in NYC!

PIZZA - FLATBREAD

The Todd English Food Hall
www.theplazany.com/dining/todd-english-food-hall

1 West 59th Street
(in The Plaza Hotel)
New York, NY 10019
(212) 986-9260

The Classic flatbread pizza at The Todd English Food Hall is super thin and has a crisp crust. It is very light, and the pizza comes out in an oval shape. There are several flavors offered, but I prefer The Classic – this one has sweet roasted tomato sauce and fresh mozzarella and basil. All the ingredients come together to make a great flatbread pizza.

Barbounia

www.barbounia.com

250 Park Avenue South
(at 20th Street)
New York, NY 10003
(212) 995-0242

PIZZA - REGULAR NYC SLICE

Joe's Pizza
www.joespizzanyc.com

7 Carmine Street
(between Avenue Of The Americas & Minetta Lane)
New York, NY 10014
(212) 366-1182

150 East 14th Street
(between Irving Place & Third Avenue)
New York, NY 10003
(212) 388-9474

Whenever I go to the West Village, I always stop to get a perfect slice of pizza at Joe's Pizza. Joe's only sells a few types of pizza including a plain slice and a Sicilian slice. The plain slice is very thin. It comes directly out of the oven and is super, super hot. The first time I tried it, I made the mistake of taking a small bite of pizza just after I had been handed a slice; it burned my mouth. The slice is not at all doughy, but has a crispy layer of cheese on it. The sauce is very light and delicious. Overall, it is an impeccable slice of pizza.

Lombardi's
www.firstpizza.com

32 Spring Street
(between Mott & Mulberry Streets)
New York, NY 10012
(212) 941-7994

Lombardi's has amazingly delicious pizza made in a coal-burning oven (which they claim is even older than the restaurant itself!). It has a thin crust, but not so thin that it breaks apart. There are many toppings to choose from, but the plain version is my favorite. It is topped with a wonderful red sauce that tastes sweet and fresh, as well as circles of sizzling fresh mozzarella cheese. The overall taste is more sauce than cheese, which I find very pleasing. When you bite into the pizza, all the flavors come together in your mouth and urge you to take another bite. The pizza is not heavy, and not overwhelmingly spicy, so you really will want to eat a lot of it. It is truly a taste sensation.

RUNNER UP
Di Fara Pizza

www.difara.com

1424 Avenue J
(at East 15th Street)
Brooklyn, NY 11230
(718) 258-1367

RUNNER UP
Luzzo's

www.luzzosgroup.com/luzzos-group-restaurants/luzzos

211 First Avenue
(between 12th & 13th Streets)
New York, NY 10003
(212) 473-7447

PIZZA - SICILIAN SQUARE

L&B Spumoni Gardens

www.spumonigardens.com

2725 86th Street
(between West 10th & 11th Streets)
Brooklyn, NY 11223
(718) 449-6921

The plain pizza squares here simply have no equal. The pizza crust on the squares is thick, with soft dough. When you take a bite, the freshness of the tomato sauce jumps right out at you and you feel yourself digging into the delicious breading. Somehow, the cheese seems to be mixed right into the sauce but each bite seems light. You have to taste this pizza to believe it. Even if you normally aren't a big fan of Sicilian pizza, you won't be able to resist these incredible pizza squares. These squares definitely are amazing and a NYC treasure!

Two Boots Pizzeria

www.twoboots.com

1617 Second Avenue
(at East 84th Street)
New York, NY 10028
(212) 734-0317

201 West 11th Street
(between Waverly Place & Greenwich Avenue)
New York, NY 10014
(212) 633-9096

2547 Broadway
(between 95th & 96th Streets)
New York, NY 10025
(212) 280-2668

42 Avenue A
(between 3rd & 4th Streets)
New York, NY 10009
(212) 254-1919

514 2nd Street
(between Seventh & Eighth Avenues)
Brooklyn, NY 11215
(718) 499-3253

625 Ninth Avenue
(between 44th & 45th Streets)
New York, NY 10036
(212) 956-2668

74 Bleecker Street
(at Broadway)
New York, NY 10012
(212) 777-1033

Grand Central - Lower Level
(between 42nd Street & Vanderbilt Avenue)
New York, NY 10017
(212) 557-7992

Two Boots Pizzeria is a cool place that started in the East Village. The "two boots" stand for the boot shape of Italy and the boot shape of Louisiana. The plain pizza is very tasty, but my personal favorite is the Bayou Beast, which features crawfish and Cajun sausage. Some people can't handle the spiciness of the slice, but keep in mind that you can always order the pizza with "plain" non-spicy sauce. As an added bonus, all of the Two Boots pizzerias are super kid-friendly.

RUNNER UP

California Pizza Kitchen

www.cpk.com

440 Park Avenue South
(between 29th & 30th Streets)
New York, NY 10016
(212) 685-6700

PULLED PORK SANDWICH

Num Pang
www.numpangnyc.com

28 East 12th Street
(between Fifth Avenue & University Place)
New York, NY 10003
(646) 791-0439

148 W 48th Street
(between Sixth and Seventh Avenues)
New York, NY 10036
(212) 421-0743

140 East 41st Street
(between Lexington & Third Avenue)
New York, NY 10017
(212) 867-8889

1129 Broadway
(between West 25th & 26th Streets)
New York, NY 10010
(212) 647-8889

75 Ninth Avenue
(between West 15th and 16th Streets)
New York, NY 10011
(213) 390-8851

225 Liberty Street
(at Vesey Street)
New York, NY 10281
(212) 227-1957

75 Broad Street
(entrance on South William Street)
New York, NY 10004
(646) 964-4150

200 Water Street
(between John and Fulton Streets)
New York, NY 10038
(917) 475-1854

The Pulled Pork sandwich at Num Pang is unlike any other pulled pork sandwich I've ever eaten. On a perfectly toasted baguette-like oval roll lies a delicious layer of sweet and sour, tender pulled pork. On top of the pulled pork is a light creamy spicy mayo spread. I like to add pickled carrots and take a refreshing bite of the cold cucumber with some cilantro. All in all, it is an incredible mixture of flavorful ingredients in an unforgettable sandwich.

RIBS

Daisy May's BBQ USA
www.daisymaysbbq.com

623 Eleventh Avenue
(at 46th Street)
New York, NY 10036
(212) 977-1500

The Kansas City sweet and sticky pork ribs are the standout at Daisy May's BBQ USA. They are sweet and gooey, and when you take a bite, your teeth sink into the lean rib meat. In fact, there is barely any fat on these ribs at all, which is something I really appreciate in a rib. The ribs themselves have lots of meat on them and the best tasting sauce ever. If you love ribs, you have got to find your way to Daisy May's!

SALAD - CAESAR

Pietro's
www.pietrosnyc.com

232 East 43rd Street
(between Second & Third Avenues)
New York, NY 10017
(212) 682-9760

After trying the Caesar salad at Pietro's, I realized I had found the perfect Caesar salad! It was delicious. The salad has a little bit of tang from the anchovies cut up in the salad. There are also tiny, crunchy croutons on the salad. I normally don't love croutons, but the ones on the Caesar salad at Pietro's are especially tasty. There is also a lot of parmesan cheese in the salad that adds a nice texture to the fresh romaine lettuce. Unlike some of the other Caesar salads that I have tried, the Pietro's Caesar does not have a watery dressing. Overall, Pietro's mixes a ton of ingredients together to make an excellent Caesar salad.

SALAD - COBB

Redeye Grill
www.redeyegrill.com

890 Seventh Avenue
(at 56th Street)
New York, NY 10019
(212) 541-9000

Redeye Grill claims that its Cobb salad is "world famous." That might be a slight exaggeration, but one thing is for sure, Redeye Grill's Cobb salad is really good. Served on an enormous platter piled high with delicious grilled chicken, nice tomatoes, crisp bacon, fresh avocado, chopped egg, blue cheese, and other great toppings, it's a meal in itself – and a memorable one at that. If you or anyone in your family likes Cobb salad, Redeye is a great place to go. [Just one hint: I would decline the offer to have the server mix it for you at your table, and would also order the dressing on the side so you can decide exactly how much you want of each ingredient in every bite.]

RUNNER UP

New York Burger Co.

www.newyorkburgerco.com

470 West 23rd Street
(at Tenth Avenue)
New York, NY 10011
(212) 255-0400

678 Sixth Avenue
(between 21st & 22nd Streets)
New York, NY 10010
(212) 229-1404

SALAD - GRILED CHICKEN

Ranch One
www.ranchone.com

110 Pearl Street
(between Water & Stone Streets)
New York, NY 10005
(212) 232-0003

Surprisingly, Ranch One, a fast-food restaurant, has a terrific grilled chicken salad. The chicken comes in thin, grilled strips. It is perfectly cooked: you can see the grill marks on the still-moist chicken. From the greens to the small crumbles of goat cheese on top, all of the ingredients in the salad are fresh. This is definitely the best fast food salad you will ever eat, and one of the best grilled chicken salads you will have – period.

STEAK

Del Frisco's
www.delfriscos.com

1221 Avenue of the Americas
(between 48th & 49th Streets)
New York, NY 10020
(212) 575-5129

At Del Frisco's, every meal feels like a party. The restaurant is huge, loud and fun, and the servers are very friendly. But the best part of Del Frisco's is the food, especially the mouthwatering steaks. I like the filet mignon the best — it is lean and also very flavorful as a result of its delicious seasoning. The steak is also very juicy. No matter how you like your steak, the restaurant will cook it to perfection. The key to these delicious steaks is the impeccable seasoning. Del Frisco's also has very good side dishes. My favorites are the chateau potatoes (a delicious pile of gooey, cheesy potatoes), the spinach supreme (creamed spinach), and the lobster macaroni and cheese (a meal in itself).

RUNNER UP

Peter Luger Steak House

www.peterluger.com

178 Broadway
(at Driggs Avenue)
Brooklyn, NY 11211
(718) 387-7400

RUNNER UP

Strip House

www.striphouse.com

13 East 12th Street
(between Fifth Avenue & University Place)
New York, NY 10003
(212) 328-0000

11 East 12th Street
(between Fifth Avenue & University Place)
New York, NY 10003
(212) 838-9197

15 West 44th Street
(between Fifth & Sixth Avenue)
New York, NY 10036
(212) 336-5454

TUNA SALAD SANDWICH

Eisenberg's Sandwich Shop
www.eisenbergsnyc.com

174 Fifth Avenue
(between 22nd & 23rd Streets)
New York, NY 10010
(212) 675-5096

I am not one to brag about tuna sandwiches, but this is one of the best tuna sandwiches I have ever eaten. I like to have mine on fresh white bread. The tuna is creamy, but not too creamy, and it doesn't even get the bread soggy. The lettuce and tomato are also really fresh. There isn't too much of any one ingredient: it is the perfect balance of flavors and textures. If you are in the mood for a really great tuna sandwich, this is the place.

TURKEY CLUB

EJ's Luncheonette
www.ejsluncheonette.com

1271 Third Avenue
(at 73rd Street)
New York, NY 10021
(212) 472-0600

Always a great family place, EJ's Luncheonette has a terrific turkey club sandwich. The turkey is thin, fresh, and delicious, and the bacon is crisp. I like mine on toasted white bread, but there is a choice of bread. The sandwich also contains a basil mayo which has a subtle taste. Light, tasty, and satisfying, this sandwich is everything you could want in a great turkey club.

RUNNER UP

Viand Cafe

www.viandcafenyc.com

2130 Broadway
(at 75th Street)
New York, NY 10023
(212) 877-2888

CHAPTER **3**

INTERNATIONAL FOODS/SPECIALTY DISHES

BAGEL SANDWICH

Russ and Daughters

www.russanddaughters.com

179 East Houston Street
(between Allen & Orchard Streets)
New York, NY 10002
(212) 475-4880

I admit that the "Super Heeb" sandwich at Russ and Daughters sounds strange (and I can see how the name might offend some, but I don't think they mean it in a bad way). I actually think you need to try this sandwich mixture in order to appreciate it. It is a bagel sandwich, stuffed with whitefish salad, wasabi roe, and horseradish cream cheese. You may not like the sound of those flavors (I didn't at first), but they blend amazingly well together, and the combination is indescribably delicious. The sandwich is a little spicy, but not mouth-burning. It is more mouthwatering. It's like nothing you have ever tasted before, and well worth a try if you are up for a little culinary adventure.

RUNNER UP

Black Seed Bagels

www.blackseedbagels.com

170 Elizabeth Street
(between Spring & Kenmare Streets)
New York, NY 10012
(212) 730-1950

200 Vesey Street
(Hudson Eats @ Brookfield Place)
New York, NY 10080
(212) 417-7000

176 First Avenue
(between 10th and 11th Streets)
New York, NY 10009
(646) 484-5718

BURRITOS

Baby Bo's Cantina
www.babyboscantinanyc.com

627 Second Avenue
(between 34th & 35th Streets)
New York, NY 10016
(212) 779-2656

The burritos at Baby Bo's Cantina are big and super stuffed. The outside of the burrito is light. I tried the super vegetarian. It is overflowing with guacamole, sour cream, rice and beans, and comes with lettuce and tomato chunks. There is also fresh salsa on the side. I love the salsa: it's pretty spicy, but I like it that way. The burrito is also excellent with tasty grilled chicken or steak in it. This is a cool restaurant, with Christmas lights up all year round. It's a great place to enjoy some awesome burritos and some warm chips and salsa.

RUNNER UP

Blockheads Burritos

www.blockheads.com

(Note: Blockheads Burritos is a really kid-friendly place. I generally like to select my own ingredients, but you might want to try Blockhead's excellent jerk chicken burrito filled with spicy jerk chicken, cheese, beans, and much more.)

1563 Second Avenue
(between 81st & 82nd Streets)
New York, NY 10028
(212) 879-1999

175 West 90th Street
(corner of 91st Street &
  Amsterdam Avenue)
New York, NY 10024
(212) 510-7410

322 West 50th Street
(between Eighth & Ninth Avenues)
New York, NY 10019
(212) 307-7029

499 Third Avenue
(between 33rd & 34th Streets)
New York, NY 10016
(212) 213-3322

954 Second Avenue
(between 50th & 51st Streets)
New York, NY 10022
(212) 750-2020

951 Amsterdam Avenue
(between 106th & 107th Streets)
New York, NY 10025
(212) 662-8226

CHEESE FONDUE

Artisanal

www.artisanalbistro.com

2 Park Avenue
(at 32nd Street)
New York, NY 10016
(212) 725-8585

Artisanal is known for its fondues. My favorite is the Artisanal Blend fondue, a mild and delicious blend of cheeses. The fondue is served with chopped baguette bread, and you can also order cut-up apples and other tasty items for dipping. The cheese has just the right amount of gooeyness and does not harden too quickly. This is a great dish to share with others and one of my absolute favorites.

La Bonne Soupe

www.labonnesoupe.com

48 West 55th Street
(between Fifth & Sixth Avenues)
New York, NY 10019
(212) 586-7650

CHICKEN PARM

Tony's Di Napoli
www.tonysnyc.com

1081 Third Avenue
(between 63rd & 64th Streets)
New York, NY 10065
(212) 888-6333

147 West 43rd Street
(between Broadway & Sixth Avenue)
New York, NY 10036
(212) 221-0100

I still think that the chicken parm at Tony's Di Napoli is the greatest. It's classic Italian fare, high-quality, but not too fancy. Tony's Di Napoli's chicken parm has an amazing tomato sauce with onions that adds some great-tasting sweetness. The chicken is tender and thin and perfectly breaded. The dish is served as it should be with spaghetti and sauce on the side. Not sure what they do to it, but this chicken parm can't be beat.

CRISPY BEEF

Philippe Chow
www.philippechow.com

33 East 60th Street
(between Madison & Park Avenues)
New York, NY 10065
(212) 644-8885

Philippe has the best crispy beef. It is crunchy, sweet, and spicy all at the same time. They bring it to you piping hot. The incredible sauce has a similar consistency to thick syrup and is very addictive. I love the sauce so much that when I'm finished with the crispy strips of beef, I pour the sauce on some white rice to complete the dish.

Red Farm

www.redfarmnyc.com

2170 Broadway
(between West 76th & West 77th Streets)
New York, NY 10024
(212) 792-9700

529 Hudson Street
(between West 10th & Charles Streets)
New York, NY 10014
(212) 792-9700

FAJITAS

Canyon Road
www.canyonroadnyc.com

1470 First Avenue
(between 76th & 77th Streets)
New York, NY 10021
(212) 734-1600

The chicken and steak fajitas at Canyon Road are my favorite in NYC. Both the chicken and steak are excellent and come perfectly grilled and seasoned. The slices of chicken and steak are thin and the fajitas are served with really tasty salsa, as well as the other essentials: great guacamole, fresh sour cream, and tasty rice and beans. The tortillas are the perfect consistency – not too flimsy to hold the filling in, but definitely not too thick as to dominate the dish. You really don't want to taste the tortilla too much. There are a few veggies (like carrots) thrown into the normal mixture of grilled onions and peppers, but you can pick them out if you don't want them. All in all, excellent fajitas.

RUNNER UP

Cilantro

www.cilantronyc.com

485 Columbus Avenue
(between 83rd & 84th Streets)
New York, NY 10024
(212) 712-9090

1321 First Avenue
(between 70th & 71st Streets)
New York, NY 10021
(212) 537-4040

RUNNER UP

Gabriela's

www.gabrielas.com

688 Columbus Avenue
(between 93rd & 94th Streets)
New York, NY 10025
(212) 961-9600

Azuri Café

www.azuricafe.com

465 West 51st Street
(between Ninth & Tenth Avenues)
New York, NY 10019
(212) 262-2920

Azuri Cafe makes awesome falafel. Served in a thick pita (that won't easily leak) with really fresh veggies and an appropriate amount of tasty sauce, Azuri Cafe's falafel sandwich has the perfect crunch. In short, their falafel is ridiculously good and not to be missed if you are a falafel fan.

Mamoun's Falafel Restaurant

www.mamouns.com

119 MacDougal Street
(between Bleecker & West Third Streets)
New York, NY 10012
(212) 674-8685

22 Saint Marks Place
(between Second & Third Avenues)
New York, NY 10003
(212) 387-7747

RUNNER UP

Taim

www.taimfalafel.com

222 Waverly Place
(between Perry & West 11th Streets)
New York, NY 10014
(212) 691-1287

FRENCH ONION SOUP

Café Centro
http://www.patinagroup.com/cafe-centro

200 Park Avenue
(at 45th Street)
New York, NY 10166
(212) 818-1222

Café Centro's version of French onion soup comes in a huge bowl, covered with beautifully-browned and bubbly melted cheese, just the right texture – not too thick and not too thin to hold up to your happily digging spoon. Underneath the baked cheese cover is a tasty, hot onion broth that contains a piece or two of soft French bread, lots of soft, sweet onions and some more gooey melted cheese.

RUNNER UP
Strip House

www.striphouse.com

13 East 12th Street
(between Fifth Avenue & University Place)
New York, NY 10003
(212) 328-0000

15 West 44th Street
(between Fifth & Sixth Avenue)
New York, NY 10036
(212) 336-5454

11 East 12th Street
(between Fifth Avenue & University Place)
New York, NY 10003
(212) 838-9197

RUNNER UP
Artisanal

www.artisanalbistro.com

2 Park Avenue
(at 32nd Street)
New York, NY 10016
(212) 725-8585

FRIED ZUCCHINI/EGGPLANT

Estiatorio Milos
www.estiatoriomilos.com

125 West 55th Street
(between Sixth & Seventh Avenues)
New York, NY 10019
(212) 245-7400

Estiatorio Milos's fried zucchini/eggplant (called the "Milos Special") is uniquely light and positively delicious. Served in impossibly thin, very lightly battered, coin-like shapes, the zucchini and eggplant slices are very easy to inhale. The Milos Special is served with a refreshing cucumber yogurt dip (called Tzatziki) that really brings out the flavor of the fried zucchini, and is a great dish for sharing. It might sound a little different from your normal fare, but if you want to try something really tasty, this dish is not to be missed!

GENERAL TSO'S CHICKEN

Our Place China Chalet

www.ourplace79.com

242 East 79th Street
(between Second & Third Avenues)
New York, NY 10075
(212) 288-4888

General Tso's Chicken is at the epicenter of Americanized Chinese food. The dish consists of a salty sweet sauce on top of battered and fried pieces of chicken. My favorite General Tso's chicken in NYC is the sweeter, less vinegar-tasting version from Our Place China Chalet. They really conquer the crispiness of the chicken and the delectable sauce. General Tso's at China Chalet is really great with white rice and altogether a fantastic dish.

China Fun

www.chinafun-ny.com

1221 Second Avenue
(at 64th Street)
New York, NY 10065
(212) 752-0810

GNOCCHI

Patricia's

www.patriciasnyc.com

1082 Morris Park Avenue
(between Lurting & Haight Avenues)
Bronx, NY 10461
(718) 409-9069

I went to Patricia's and had the gnocchi, which was by far my favorite gnocchi of all time. The light, delicate and soft potato dumplings are sensational. They practically melt in your mouth, and with the addition of a ton of Patricia's great, sweet tomato sauce and a lot of melted cheese, the gnocchi is, in a word, fantastic.

GUACAMOLE

Rosa Mexicano

www.rosamexicano.com

1063 First Avenue
(at 58th Street)
New York, NY 10022
(212) 753-7407

61 Columbus Avenue
(at 62nd Street)
New York, NY 10023
(212) 977-7700

9 East 18th Street
(between Fifth Avenue & Broadway)
New York, NY 10003
(212) 533-3350

You simply can't beat Rosa Mexicano's guacamole. It's made at your table in a stone bowl, and has all the best ingredients – from the fresh, ripe avocados to the perfect spices. They add heat to your liking, and it is served with warm, crispy tortilla chips. You will be in guacamole heaven here for sure!

KNISH

Yonah Schimmel Knish Bakery

137 East Houston Street
(between 1st & 2nd)
New York, NY 10002
(212) 477-2858

With no greasiness, Yonah Schimmel Knish Bakery serves up some incredibly soft and tasty potato knishes. The chewiness of the crust and the buttery, fluffy potatoes make for an incredible knish. These knishes are an authentic taste of old NYC and shouldn't be missed.

MEDITERRANEAN SPREADS

Estiatorio Milos

www.estiatoriomilos.com

125 West 55th Street
(between Sixth & Seventh Avenues)
New York, NY 10019
(212) 245-7400

The Mediterranean spreads at Milos are fantastic. From the Tzatziki (a spread made of yogurt, cucumber, garlic and olive oil) to the Skordalia (almonds, garlic) to the Htipiti (Holland peppers, feta cheese, olive oil), these are delicious and really fun to share. The spreads are served with thick, lightly grilled bread.

RUNNER UP

Barbounia

www.barbounia.com

250 Park Avenue South
(at 20th Street)
New York, NY 10003
(212) 995-0242

NACHOS

Brother Jimmy's BBQ
www.brotherjimmys.com

1 East 161st Street
(at Yankee Stadium)
Bronx, NY 10451

116 East 16th Street
(between Park Avenue South & Irving Place)
New York, NY 10003
(212) 673-6465

1485 Second Avenue
(between 77th & 78th Streets)
New York, NY 10075
(212) 288-0999

181 Lexington Avenue
(between 31st & 32nd Streets)
New York, NY 10016
(212) 779-7427

416 Eighth Avenue
(at 31st Street)
New York, NY 10001
(212) 967-7603

Brother Jimmy's nachos are piled high and come with all the best toppings: cheese, tomatoes, lettuce, fresh salsa, guacamole, beans, sour cream, and more. Their nachos have all the right flavors, and there is nothing weird in them. The nachos platter is pretty big, so if you are looking for a filling snack or an appetizer to share with friends or family, this is the place to go.

(Note: Brother Jimmy's BBQ restaurants are super kid-friendly.)

NOODLES

HanGawi
www.hangawirestaurant.com

12 East 32nd Street
(between Madison & Fifth Avenues)
New York, NY 10016
(212) 213-0077

HanGawi is a cool Korean restaurant where you get the feeling of sitting on the floor (although there are actually dug-out spaces beneath the low tables in which to dangle your feet). It is a vegan restaurant, but the food is so good and the dishes so complex and tasty, I don't even notice that all the dishes are vegan when I am eating there. My favorite dish at HanGawi is the Korean glass noodles (called Vermicelli Delight), which the menu says are made of sweet potatoes, but they taste like regular noodles. They are cooked in what looks like a thin paper bag, and when they arrive at the table, the server breaks open the paper and pours the noodles onto a serving plate. The noodles are almost clear, and they are kind of slippery with a cellophane-like texture. They arrive piping hot and steamy, and are so light and tasty, you cannot stop eating them. The noodles are mixed with a few light vegetables like delicate strips of carrots. You may find yourself fighting over these noodles!

(Note: HanGawi isn't a traditional kids' restaurant, but I have always loved going there with my parents, and the employees have been nothing but nice to my brother and me. As a special treat, on someone's birthday, they sound a big gong in the middle of the restaurant, which is something you won't easily forget.)

PEKING DUCK SLIDERS

Red Egg
www.redeggnyc.com

202 Centre Street
(at Howard Street)
New York, NY 10013
(212) 966-1123

The Peking duck sliders at Red Egg are fantastic. They make these sliders right at your table. First, they start off with a light, fresh little white bun. Then they get perfectly cooked duck with crisp skin and put it on the little white bun. Next, they add some cold cucumber and some sweet Hoisin sauce. When you bite into this slider, your teeth sink into the soft bun and then you get to the thick layer of hot duck and the cold cucumber. Plus, the sauce gives it a nice sweet flavor. The duck sliders are truly delicious.

PAD THAI

Galanga
www.galanganyc.com

149 West Fourth Street
(between Sixth Avenue & MacDougal Street)
New York, NY 10012
(212) 228-4267

The Pad Thai at Galanga is so good. Its noodles never stick together; instead, the noodles are properly firm without a gluey texture and come with the perfect amount of sauce. Also, their Pad Thai is not too packed with veggies or other extraneous ingredients. My favorite is the Pad Thai with chicken, but you can also order it with shrimp or just vegetables. The Pad Thai at Galanga has a combination of so many great flavors including spices melded with finely chopped peanuts and such hot noodles that you may never want to stop eating it. If Pad Thai is something you enjoy, you will definitely love this Pad Thai!

RUNNER UP

Jaiya Thai

www.jaiya.com

396 Third Avenue
(at 28th Street)
New York, NY 10016
(212) 889-1330

1553 Second Avenue
(between East 80th and 81st Streets)
New York, NY 10028
(212) 717-8877

La Paella

www.lapaellanyc.com

214 East Ninth Street
(between Second & Third Avenues)
New York, NY 10003
(212) 598-4321

The Basque Paella at La Paella is awesome. It has perfectly cooked rice, peas, mussels, clams, sausage, shrimp, and chicken. All the great flavors mix together, and you can sink your teeth into the moist chicken, fresh seafood, and nicely cooked sausage. You will love the spiced rice and peas as well. This is a great dish, with an interesting flavor, which is served hot and cooked just right. This paella definitely makes for a delicious and satisfying meal.

La Nacional

www.facebook.com/LaNacionalTapasNYC

239 West 14th Street
(between Seventh & Eighth Avenues)
New York, NY 10011
(212) 243-9308

PIEROGI

Vaselka
www.veselka.com

144 Second Avenue
(between St. Marks Place & Ninth Street)
New York, NY 10003
(212) 228-9682

Vaselka has some of the best pierogis (Polish dumplings) you can find anywhere. There are several varieties including cheese and potato, and you can order them boiled or fried. I am a fan of both the cheese and the potato dumplings. The cheese dumplings are soft, fluffy and delicate and best eaten with Vaselka's caramelized onions and apple sauce. I like both the boiled and fried cheese dumplings, but prefer the fried ones overall and find them pleasantly non-greasy. But, the standouts for me are the potato dumplings. The boiled potato dumpling is soft and gnocci-like, while the fried potato dumpling has a pleasantly starchy flavor and a good semi-crunchy bite. If you like pierogis, you must try Vaselka's for their authentic and delicious dumplings.

PORK BUNS

Our Place China Chalet

www.ourplace79.com

242 East 79th Street
(between Second & Third Avenues)
New York, NY 10075
(212) 288-4888

The soft white buns filled with sweet roast pork are incredibly fluffy, light and tasty at Our Place China Chalet. They are small buns with the perfect amount of pork. With three to an order, you might need to consider several orders of buns because they are that good and tend to disappear very quickly.

Red Egg

www.redeggnyc.com

202 Centre Street
(at Howard Street)
New York, NY 10013
(212) 966-1123

PORK AND CHIVE DUMPLING

Northern Tiger

www.northerntigernyc.com

225 Liberty Street
(at Hudson Eats)
New York, NY 10281
(212) 786-0316

Northern Tiger is home to some of the best dumplings in all of NYC. It is unbelievable how good the pork and chive pan fried dumplings taste. They have the perfect levels of juiciness and saltiness. The chive adds a delicious complex flavor, with a sublime ratio of filling to dumpling. The pan-fried wrapper is cooked to perfection. With some citrusy-soy sauce, their dumplings are worthy of being named the best in NYC.

RAMEN

Totto Ramen
www.tottoramen.com

366 West 52nd Street
(between Eighth & Ninth Avenues)
New York, NY 10019
(212) 582-0052

248 East 52nd Street
(between Second & Third Avenues)
New York, NY 10022
(212) 421-0052

464 West 51st Street
(between Ninth & Tenth Avenues)
New York, NY 10019
(646) 596-9056

I have tried many ramens in my life inside and outside of NYC, and Totto Ramen is one of my favorites. I had the Haitan ramen which has an incredible salty flavor, and features tonkotsu noodles. Also, there is a great flavor from the pork. The green scallions play an important role in the depth of the flavor of this thicker-than-usual broth. The ramen dishes at Totto have an excellent ratio of soup to noodles, and most varieties include tasty shredded pork as well as charsiu pork circles. It is a small restaurant so there may be a wait, but it is definitely well worth it.

RUNNER UP
Ippudo Ramen

www.ippudony.com

65 Fourth Avenue
(between 9th & 10th Streets)
New York, NY 10003
(212) 388-0088

321 West 51st Street
(between Eighth & Ninth Avenues)
New York, NY 10019
(212) 974-2500

RUNNER UP
Naruto Ramen

www.narutoramenex.com

1596 Third Avenue
(between 89th & 90th Streets)
New York, NY 10128
(212) 289-7803

SHRIMP DUMPLING

Red Farm
www.redfarmnyc.com

2170 Broadway
(between West 76th & West 77th Streets)
New York, NY 10024
(212) 792-9700

529 Hudson Street
(between West 10th & Charles Streets)
New York, NY 10014
(212) 792-9700

The shrimp dumplings at Red Farm are very similar to the shrimp dumplings that were at Chinatown Brasserie (which closed a while back). That is most likely because Joe Ng, the old chef at Chinatown Brasserie, has been a chef at Red Farm. The difference is that at Red Farm there are four different types of shrimp dumplings in each order. The four delicious flavors are: the white, plain original shrimp dumpling; the yellow dumpling that seems to have chopped up mushrooms; the blue shrimp dumpling; and the spicy red shrimp dumpling. The wrapper on these shrimp dumplings is super thin and light. The sauce that comes with the dish is like a soy sauce, with a little more spice. Finally, this awesome dumpling dish is served with a delicious fried sweet potato in the shape of a "Pac-Man." In short, this is a fun, tasty dish that is perfect for adventurous kids and adults who like shrimp and can handle some spice.

SOUP DUMPLING

The Bao
no website

13 St. Marks Place
(between Second and Third Avenues)
New York, NY 10003
(212) 388-9238

I went to try the soup dumplings at the Bao and was pleasantly surprised. They have a large variety of soup dumplings including wasabi, chocolate, super spicy crab and regular pork. The soup dumplings all have an ultra-thin wrapper except for the chocolate which has a gooier crepe-like wrapper. I really enjoy the large amount of soup in the dumplings and the soft delicate meat in the middle of all of the dumplings (except for the chocolate which has a thin cut of mushy banana in the center). My favorites are the wasabi dumplings, which have a kick of spice in them that complements the saltiness of the soup and the chewiness of the pork. Overall, The Bao is a good find and I highly recommend the soup dumplings there.

RUNNER UP
Joe's Shanghai

www.joeshanghairestaurants.com

24 West 56th Street
(between Fifth Avenue & Avenue Of The Americas)
New York, NY 10019
(212) 333-3868

RUNNER UP
Red Farm

www.redfarmnyc.com

2170 Broadway
(between West 76th & West 77th Streets)
New York, NY 10024
(212) 792-9700

529 Hudson Street
(between West 10th & Charles Streets)
New York, NY 10014
(212) 792-9700

Sushi Nakazawa

www.sushinakazawa.com

23 Commerce Street
(between South Seventh Avenue & Bedford Street)
New York, NY 10014
(212) 924-2212

I waited many months to go to Sushi Nakazawa. With reservations at the sushi bar being nearly impossible to get, I finally got a reservation in the main room. As an aside, I have done lots of research on Sushi Nakazawa, a disciple of the famous Jiro Ono, and was outrageously excited and ecstatic to go there. Sushi has become one of my favorite foods, so I've been very interested in sushi lately, and the hype for Sushi Nakazawa was ridiculous, adding another layer of excitement. The meal is a 20 piece nigiri omakase (chef's choice) with the addition of sorbet and a cup of matcha tea for dessert. The 20 piece nigiri omakase is the only menu option, and the menu changes based on the availability of the fish.

When I got to Sushi Nakazawa, I walked past Chef Nakazawa on my way to the small back room. Then, in close time intervals, I received seven courses of a few pieces of nigiri and one course of sorbet and tea. A perfect evolution from one course to the next made this meal impeccable and exceeded my expectations. The differences in textures and consistency of the fish and the different sauces and toppings gave each course a certain level of creativity and added some excitement as I wondered what would come next. My favorite courses were the unexplainably creamy uni (sea urchin), and the tamago (egg omelet) which is amazingly cake-like. All I can say is what an incredible experience it is to eat sushi at Sushi Nakazawa. I highly recommend it to any serious sushi lover.

(Note: If you are super hungry and looking for a more filling dinner, you may want to choose one of the runner-ups as Sushi Nakazawa only serves around 20 pieces.)

Sasabune

www.sasabunenyc.com

401 East 73rd Street
(between First & York Avenues)
New York, NY
212 249-8583

Runner Up listings continued on next page...

SUSHI

RUNNER UP

Soto

www.sotonyc.com

345 East 12th Street
(between West Fourth Street & Washington Place)
New York, NY 10014
(212) 414-3088

RUNNER UP

Sushi Yasuda

www.sushiyasuda.com

(Note: A super incredible experience at the Sushi bar.)

204 East 43rd Street
(between Second & Third Avenues)
New York, NY 10017
(212) 972-1001

VEGGIE DUMPLING

China Fun

www.chinafun-ny.com

1221 Second Avenue
(at 64th Street)
New York, NY 10065
(212) 752-0810

I tried many different veggie dumplings all around the city, and my favorite are the classic green vegetable dumplings at China Fun. The green dough-like casing on these vegetable dumplings is thick and soft. The inside consists of lots of tiny chopped up pieces of vegetables. Then, to top them off, there is a delicious sweet and salty sauce. The result is one great dumpling that never disappoints.

RUNNER UP

Red Egg

www.redeggnyc.com

202 Centre Street
(at Howard Street)
New York, NY 10013
(212) 966-1123

RUNNER UP

Vanessa's Dumpling House

www.vanessasdumplinghouse.com

118 Eldridge Street
(between Grand & Broome Streets)
New York, NY 10002
(212) 625-8008

220 East 14th Street
(between Second & Third Avenues)
New York, NY 10003
(212) 529-1329

310 Bedford Avenue
(between South First & Second Streets)
Brooklyn, NY 11211
(212) 734-7441

CHAPTER 4

SEAFOOD DISHES

GRILLED FISH

Estiatorio Milos

www.estiatoriomilos.com

125 West 55th Street
(between Sixth & Seventh Avenues)
New York, NY 10019
(212) 245-7400

Estiatorio Milos is a high-ceilinged restaurant known for its incredibly fresh seafood – which is generally priced by the pound. While this is a sophisticated restaurant, it is certainly welcoming to families with kids. They have some big round tables, which are especially good for larger groups. With permission from the wait staff, you can actually take a stroll up to the fish, which are displayed on an enormous pile of shaved ice. No matter what your age, they might even prod you to go up there and take a look – they seem really proud of their fish. My favorite fish at Milos is the branzino, which I always share with someone. The fish comes simply grilled and has a really delicious, non-fishy flavor. You have to order the side dishes separately, but they are also amazing, especially the lemon potatoes and the crisp French fries.

Oceana

www.oceanarestaurant.com

120 West 49th Street
(between Sixth & Seventh Avenues)
New York, NY 10020
(212) 759-5941

LOBSTER ROLL

Mary's Fish Camp
www.marysfishcamp.com

64 Charles Street
(at West Fourth Street)
New York, NY 10014
(646) 486-2185

The lobster roll at Mary's Fish Camp is exceptional, totally fresh, and delectable. You can have similar lobster rolls at other places, but they won't have precisely the same well-balanced and creamy texture. The way all the seasonings and butteriness and creaminess come together is just amazing. Furthermore, unlike the lobster rolls at some other places, the lobster salad served on the rolls at Mary's Fish Camp includes all the best parts of the lobster, including lots of lobster tail. In addition, the bun is buttery, and virtually melts in your mouth, which is so important in a great lobster roll. There are other good ones in the city, but Mary's has simply perfected the lobster roll. Give it a try, and you'll see what I mean.

RUNNER UP
Ditch Plains

www.ditch-plains.com

29 Bedford Street
(at Downing Street)
New York, NY 10014
(212) 633-0202

RUNNER UP
Ed's Lobster Bar

www.lobsterbarnyc.com

222 Lafayette Street
(between Kenmare & Spring Streets)
New York, NY 10012
(212) 343-3236

MUSSELS

B. Café
www.bcafe.com

566 Amsterdam Avenue
(between 87th & 88th Streets)
New York, NY 10024
(212) 873-0003

240 East 75th Street
(between Second & Third Avenues)
New York, NY 10021
(212) 249-3300

In an almost hidden spot on an Upper Eastside street, B. Café is serving up some of the best mussels in NYC. B. Café is an institution. I love the Provencale Mussels dish which has such a good sauce I drank all of the remaining sauce after finishing the mussels. The tomato based broth has very light tomato sweetness and a saltiness that makes the remarkable small mussels very, very tasty. I can eat multiple plates of these mussels. Accompanied with some fries, the delicious mussels are the star of the show.

RUNNER UP
Brasserie Magritte

www.brasseriemagritte.com

1463 Third Avenue
(between 82nd & 83rd Streets)
New York, NY 10028
(646) 449-0606

RUNNER UP
Flex Mussels

www.flexmusselsny.com

154 West 13th Street
(between Sixth & Seventh Avenues)
New York, NY 10011
(212) 229-0222

174 East 82nd Street
(between Lexington & Third Avenues)
New York, NY 10028
(212) 717-7772

NEW ENGLAND CLAM CHOWDER

Pearl Oyster Bar

www.pearloysterbar.com

18 Cornelia Street
(between Bleecker & West Fourth Streets)
New York, NY 10014
(212) 691-8211

Pearl Oyster Bar continues to feature great clam chowder. It is light and creamy and packed with spices that are hard to identify, but wonderful. The chowder has nice potatoes and well-cooked clams that are small and not too chewy. The chowder arrives super-hot, so you will need to let it cool down for a while before you can really dig in. I tried many bowls of chowder, but Pearl Oyster Bar's is special. Give it a try!

RUNNER UP

Ed's Chowder House

www.chinagrillmgt.com

44 West 63rd Street
(inside The Empire Hotel)
New York, NY 10023
(212) 956-1288

SHRIMP ROLL

Luke's Lobster
www.lukeslobster.com

242 East 81st Street
(between Second & Third Avenues)
New York, NY 10028
(212) 249-4241

26 South William Street
(at Stone Street)
New York, NY 10004
(212) 747-1700

426 Amsterdam Avenue
(between 80th & 81st Streets)
New York, NY 10024
(212) 877-8800

93 East Seventh Street
(between Avenue A & First Avenue)
New York, NY 10009
(212) 387-8487

1 West 59th Street
The Plaza Food Hall
(between Fifth and Sixth Avenues)
New York, NY 10019
(646) 755-3227

207 E. 43rd St
(between Second and Third Avenues)
New York, NY 10017
(646) 657-0066

237 Fifth Avenue
(between President and Carroll Street)
New York, NY 10016
(347) 457-6855

700 Eighth Avenue
(on 2nd floor of The Row Hotel)
New York, NY 10036
(917) 338-0928

5 West 25th Street
(at Broadway)
New York, NY 10010
(646) 657-0747

The shrimp roll at Luke's Lobster has a buttery and perfectly toasted bun that melts in your mouth. Inside the bun, you will find piles of fresh shrimp with lemon and some great seasonings. The shrimp rolls at Luke's Lobster are a good size – big enough not to be skimpy, but not so huge that they are impossible to finish. When you bite into these shrimp rolls, you will feel and hear the crunch of the warm roll and then sink your teeth into the refreshingly cold shrimp. Unbelievable!

CHAPTER **5**

DESSERTS/BAKED
GOODS

APPLE/PEAR TURNOVER

La Pain Quotidien
www.lepainquotidien.com

Numerous locations throughout NYC

The Apple Pear Turnover at Le Pain Quotidien is baked to perfection. It is crispy and sweet in the best sense of the word. In the middle, there is a light apple and pear jelly-like mixture, which is covered by layers of crispy, buttery goodness. The secret to eating these is to make sure you have a piece of the sugary topping in each bite. You will need to buy two of these. Yes, they are that good!!!

BANANA PUDDING

Magnolia Bakery
www.magnoliabakery.com

401 Bleecker Street
(at West 11th Street)
New York, NY 10014
(212) 462-2572

1240 Avenue of the Americas
(at 49th Street – Rockefeller Center)
New York, NY 10020
(212) 767-1123

200 Columbus Avenue
(at 69th Street)
New York, NY 10023
(212) 724-8101

1000 Third Avenue
(inside Bloomingdales)
New York, NY 10022
(212) 265-5320

Grand Central Terminal
(Lower Dining Concourse)
New York, NY 10017
(212) 682-3588

I went to Magnolia Bakery to get a famous cupcake, but I also decided to try their banana pudding – a food I really like. The pudding there is unreal. It has a perfect sweet banana flavor with pieces of smooth, mushy, delicious banana in it. It also has crumbled up pieces of vanilla cookies that turn into vanilla cake-like pieces. All the ingredients combined made for an unforgettable and easily inhaled dessert or snack.

BANANA SPLIT

The Chocolate Room
www.thechocolateroombrooklyn.com

269 Court Street
(between Butler & Douglass Streets)
Brooklyn, NY 11231
(718) 246-2600

51 Fifth Avenue
(between St. Marks Avenue & Bergen Street)
Brooklyn, NY 11217
(718) 783-2900

The Chocolate Room has an absolutely scrumptious banana split. The key for me is the flambéed bananas with a crispy topping, which are sweet and crunchy. The cooked bananas put this banana split over the top and make it really special. The banana split at The Chocolate Room is served with chocolate, strawberry, and vanilla ice creams, which are covered in chocolate, caramel, and strawberry sauces. The sundae is topped with some whipped cream. As a whole, you have cold ice cream along with crunchy warm bananas and fluffy whipped cream. Banana splits just don't get any better.

RUNNER UP

Blue Ribbon Bakery Kitchen

www.blueribbonrestaurants.com

35 Downing Street
(at Bedford Street)
New York, NY 10014
(212) 337-0404

BEIGNET

Cafemarie
(no website)

120 MacDougal Street
(between Bleecker & West 3rd Streets)
New York, NY 10012
(212) 995-0400

This shop opened not too long ago and serves incredibly fluffy, giant beignets similar to the authentic beignets in New Orleans. These are not oily at all, with an appropriately heavy amount of powdered sugar — just unforgettable. While they come only three to an order, they are pretty large beignets so you might want to bring a friend so you can share them. By far the best beignets in NYC!

BLONDIE

Blondies Sports
www.blondiessports.com

212 West 79th Street
(between Amsterdam Avenue & Broadway)
New York, NY 10024
(212) 362-4360

I guess it is only logical that Blondies Sports would serve great blondies. The blondies there are big. They are served super-hot, and are moist and chewy. They also come with melted chocolate. You can really sink your teeth into one of these. Just beware — they have nuts in them, so don't order them if you don't like nuts or are allergic to them.

BREAD

Maison Kayser
www.maison-kayser-usa.com

1800 Broadway
(between Columbus Circle & 58th Street)
New York, NY 10019
(212) 245-4100

8 West 40th Street
(at Fifth Avenue)
New York, NY 10018
(212) 354-2300

355 Greenwich Street
(at Harrison Street)
New York, NY 10013
(212) 966-3200

1294 Third Avenue
(at East 74th Street)
New York, NY 10021
(212) 744-3100

326 Bleecker Street
(at Christopher Street)
New York, NY 10014
(212) 645-7900

2161 Broadway
(at West 76th Street)
New York, NY 10024
(212) 873-5900

921 Broadway
(at East 21st Street)
New York, NY 10010
(212) 979-1600

1513 Third Avenue
(between East 86th and 87th Streets)
New York, NY 10028
(212) 348-8400

Maison Kayser is a bakery from France that serves some unbelievable breads. The sweet, white chocolate-filled white chocolate bread fulfills any sugar craving. The delicate, soft bread is a real treat. I also like the olive bread, which has salty and sour slices of olive throughout, as well as a chewy, slightly crispy crust. Great bread!

BROWNIE

Fat Witch Bakery

www.fatwitch.com

75 Ninth Avenue
(between 15th & 16th Streets)
New York, NY 10011
(888) 419-4824

Fat Witch Bakery has many varieties of brownies. I have tried a bunch of them. The plain brownies at Fat Witch Bakery are very good. The top is gooey and the bottom is crispy like a brownie pie. They are rich, but not too rich. But, the brownie that consistently blows me away is the peppermint brownie. It is like nothing I have ever tasted – it tastes like candy canes mixed with a mound of moist chocolate. The top of the brownie is key as it is super crunchy and adds a great texture to the brownies. If you like peppermint, you've got to try it.

RUNNER UP

Dylan's Candy Bar

www.dylanscandybar.com

1011 Third Avenue
(between 60th & 61st Streets)
New York, NY 10021
(646) 735-0078

CANNOLI

Ferrara

www.ferraranyc.com

195 Grand Street
(between Mulberry & Mott Streets)
New York, NY 10013
(212) 226-6150

The cream inside the cannoli shells at Ferarra is the key. No other bakery or restaurant has the same caliber of delicious, thick and perfectly sweet dense cream. With some chocolate chips and a crunchy shell, this cannoli is unbeatable. Also, I really like the chocolate-covered cannoli too, which is a cannoli shell covered in super rich chocolate and then stuffed with cream.

RUNNER UP

Paticceria Rocco

www.roccos.nyc

243 Bleecker Street
(between Carmine & Leroy Streets)
New York, NY 10014
(212) 242-6031

CHEESECAKE

F. Monteleone Bakery and Cafe
www.fmonteleonebakery.com

355 Court Street
(between Union & President Streets)
Brooklyn, NY 11231
(718) 852-5600

F. Monteleone Bakery and Cafe cheesecakes are really special. They are creamy without being too gooey. All of them are delectable. I especially like the chocolate cheesecake. It's not dark chocolate, but has a really light chocolate flavor that is deeply delicious. If you enjoy cheesecake, this is well worth the trip.

RUNNER UP
Eileen's

www.eileenscheesecake.com

17 Cleveland Place
(corner of Kenmare & Centre Streets)
New York, NY 10012
(212) 966-5585

RUNNER UP
Junior's

www.juniorscheesecake.com

1515 Broadway
(at 44th Street)
New York, NY 10036
(212) 302-2000

386 Flatbush Avenue Extension
(at Dekalb Avenue)
Brooklyn, NY 11201
(718) 852-5257

CHOCOLATE CAKE

The Palm
www.thepalm.com

206 West Street
(between Warren & Chambers Streets)
New York, NY 10013
(646) 395-6393

250 West 50th Street
(between Eighth Avenue & Broadway)
New York, NY 10019
(212) 333-7256

840 Second Avenue
(at 45th Street)
New York, NY 10017
(212) 697-5198

I tried a lot of NYC chocolate cakes. There are many varieties. Some are more like dark chocolate tortes, but those are not for me. If you love classic chocolate cake that is not too rich and has a mouth-watering milk chocolate flavor, The Palm is the place to go. They serve a delicious, humongous slice of multi-layered chocolate cake. The Palm's chocolate cake seems to contain sweet chunks of fudge, which makes each bite especially moist and flavorful. The icing on the cake is an even richer and creamier chocolate. This cake is super delicious and great with vanilla ice cream on the side.

RUNNER UP

Del Frisco's Double Eagle Steak House

www.delfriscos.com

1221 Avenue of the Americas
(between 48th & 49th Streets)
New York, NY 10020
(212) 575-5129

CHOCOLATE FONDUE

 **Blue Water Grill**

www.bluewatergrillnyc.com

31 Union Square West
(at 16th Street)
New York, NY 10003
(212) 675-9500

When it comes to chocolate fondue, I like this one the best. The chocolate is not dark – it is a creamy, smooth milk chocolate. It is a big portion, and comes with a lot of "stuff" – marshmallows, strawberries, bananas, and more. It has the perfect amount of toppings, so it is great for sharing!

RUNNER UP

Dylan's Candy Bar

www.dylanscandybar.com

1011 Third Avenue
(between 60th & 61st Streets)
New York, NY 10021
(646) 735-0078

CHOCOLATE PIZZA

Max Brenner

www.maxbrenner.com

841 Broadway
(between 13th & 14th Streets)
New York, NY 10003
(212) 388-0030

A really amazing creation is the chocolate pizza at Max Brenner, which has a thin layer of dough and is covered with chocolate and either marshmallows or crispies (you choose from the two varieties). The pizza is served warm and round like a regular pizza pie, and is served in slices. Each slice of the pizza is soft, sweet (but not overly so), rich and chocolatey. One thing I can promise you is that this dessert pizza is so good and unique, you will want to visit often.

RUNNER UP

Dylan's Candy Bar

www.dylanscandybar.com

1011 Third Avenue
(between 60th & 61st Streets)
New York, NY 10021
(646) 735-0078

CHOCOLATE SOUFFLE

Bouchon Bakery
www.bouchonbakery.com

1 Rockefeller Plaza
(across the Plaza from NBC Studios)
New York, NY 10111
(212) 782-3890

Normally, even a great soufflé needs a liquid topping to make it super moist. But the chocolate soufflé at Bouchon Bakery is so rich, chocolaty, and flavorful that I was easily able to finish the whole thing without even adding Crème Anglaise. Topped off with powdered sugar, this dessert is unbelievable. It is crisp on the outside, but once you break through the delicate shell, the inside is gooey and soft – an amazing dessert any soufflé lover will enjoy.

CHOCOLATE TREAT (UNIQUE)

Max Brenner
www.maxbrenner.com

841 Broadway
(between 13th & 14th Streets)
New York, NY 10003
(212) 388-0030

Ever had a "chocolate syringe?" Well you need to! And, as far as I know, there is only one place to get one: Max Brenner. These syringes are rich and creamy, but not too milky. And to make it even better, when you order them at the sit-down restaurant, they put gummy bears and powdered sugar on the side. Max Brenner is almost always busy, so either make a reservation or get it to go. The takeout line at the chocolate counter moves fairly quickly and is a good option. This dessert is for chocolate LOVERS only!!! You will never think of syringes in the same way.

CINNAMON BUN

Smackery's
www.schmackarys.com

345 East 12th Street
(between Eighth & Ninth Avenues)
New York, NY 10036
(646) 801-9866

This soft, doughy cinnamon bun has a great cinnamon flavor throughout due to the thick, sugary cinnamon paste. It is a big cinnamon bun with dense dough. The "Sinful Cinnamon Bun" is covered with a sweet icing, creating a terrific breakfast or dessert item.

COOKIES - CHOCOLATE CHIP

Roasting Plant
www.roastingplant.com

81 Orchard Street
(between Broome & Grand Streets)
New York, NY 10002
(212) 775-7755

75 Greenwich Avenue
(between South Seventh Avenue & 11th Street)
New York, NY 10014
(212) 775-7755

Without a doubt, Roasting Plant has the perfect cookie. The very first time I got to go try one, the cookies were fresh out of the oven. I love the thinness of the cookies, yet they still have large chocolate chunks. These cookies take you by surprise – they have the perfect amount of chewiness and are by far the best in NYC!

RUNNER UP
Boulton & Watt

www.boultonandwattnyc.com

5 Avenue A
(at First Street)
New York, NY 10009
(646) 490-6004

RUNNER UP
Smackery's

www.schmackarys.com

345 East 12th Street
(between Ninth & Eighth Avenues)
New York, NY 10036
(646) 801-9866

RUNNER UP
Levain Bakery

www.levainbakery.com

167 West 74th Street
(at Amsterdam Avenue)
New York, NY 10023
212-874-6080

2167 Frederick Douglass Blvd.
(between West 116th & 117th Streets)
New York, NY 10026
646-455-0952

COOKIES - MADELEINES

Dominique Ansel Bakery

www.dominiqueansel.com

189 Spring Street
(between Thompson & Sullivan Streets)
New York, NY 10012
(212) 219-2773

The maker of the famous cronut, Dominique Ansel, once again has made a perfect dessert. His made-to-order madeleines come either 10 or 20 to an order. The madeleines have a slightly orangey-lemon flavor that I really like. The citrus flavor gives the dessert a layer of complexity that most other madeleines fail to fulfill. The cookies are topped with powdered sugar and served hot.

RUNNER UP

L.A. Burdick Chocolate Shop and Café

www.burdickchocolate.com

5 East 20th Street
(between Broadway & Fifth Avenue)
New York, NY 10003
(212) 796-0143

COOKIES - MILK AND COOKIE SHOTS

Dominique Ansel Bakery
www.dominiqueansel.com

189 Spring Street
(between Thompson & Sullivan Streets)
New York, NY 10012
(212) 219-2773

Dominique Ansel created yet another incredible dessert when he came up with milk and cookie shots. They are chewy chocolate chunk cookie cups that are covered in warm chocolate and then filled with cold milk. Really an amazing idea and dessert.

COOKIES - "OREO" STYLE

Plenty Café
www.plentycafenewyork.com

1457 Third Avenue
(at 82nd Street)
New York, NY 10028
(212) 628-2110

Plenty has reinvented the Oreo cookie in a way that ensures that you never run out of cream filling. Putting their own twist on the well-known chocolate sandwich cookie, the bakers at Plenty take two perfect (and huge!) chocolate cookies that are sweet and crunchy and fill them with delectable sweet cream. There is so much cream on the cookie that it is the equivalent of five double-stuffed Oreos. Beware though – this is a giant cookie sandwich – way bigger than a standard Oreo. This means that if you are really hungry for a sweet and chocolaty dessert, Plenty is the place to go. Plenty also has good layer cakes and homemade Twinkies.

COOKIES - SPECIALTY

Insomnia Cookies
www.insomniacookies.com

1028 Amsterdam Avenue
(between West 110th & 111th Streets)
New York, NY 10025
(803) 771-0060

405 Amsterdam Avenue
(between West 79th & 80th Streets)
New York, NY 10024
(877) 632-6654

1579 Second Avenue
(at East 82nd Street)
New York, NY 10028
(877) 632-6654

482 Third Avenue
(at East 33rd Street)
New York, NY 10016
(212) 725-0600

237 East 53rd Street
(between Second & Third Avenues)
New York, NY 10022
(877) 632-6654

116 MacDougal Street
(between Bleeker & West 3rd Streets)
New York, NY 10012
(877) 632-6654

I love the Deluxe Chocolate Peanut Butter Cup cookie at Insomnia. It comes out hot and soft and has tons of chocolate and peanut butter. On top of the chocolate and peanut butter around the cookie, there is a giant sweet, super-hot chocolate peanut butter cup in the middle. The cookie is quite crumbly and is perfect if you are in the mood for chocolate and peanut butter. Insomnia Cookies is open very late, hence the term "insomnia." So, if you can't sleep or are up late studying or working, and really want a hot, fresh cookie, you know who to call.

RUNNER UP
Levain Bakery

www.levainbakery.com

167 West 74th Street
(at Amsterdam Avenue)
New York, NY 10023
(212) 874-6080

2167 Frederick Douglass Blvd.
(between West 116th and 117th Streets)
New York, NY 10026
(646) 455-0952

RUNNER UP
Smackery's

www.schmackarys.com

345 East 12th Street
(between Ninth & Eighth Avenues)
New York, NY 10036
(646) 801-9866

CREAM PUFFS

Beard Papa's
www.beardpapa.com

2167 Broadway
(between 77th & 76th Streets)
New York, NY 10024
(212) 799-3770

Beard Papa's is a bakery in NYC that is also in Tokyo. They have some amazing desserts. Their cream puffs are especially good. They start with a flakey puff of dough, cook it until golden brown and stuff it with delicious vanilla cream. They also can add sweet chocolate to the top of your cream puff which is called an eclair puff. Delicate and delicious, these cream puffs are great.

CREPE

Creperie NYC

www.creperienyc.com

135 Ludlow Street
(between Stanton & Rivington Streets)
New York, NY 10002
(212) 979-5521

Creperie NYC serves up some of the best crepes in NYC. It is a tiny store in NYC, with ridiculously good crepes. My favorite is "The Famous Crepe." It is a very thin, yet almost crispy crepe filled with tasty strawberries and bananas, cold ice cream and some Nutella and then topped with chocolate sauce and whipped cream. It is a fantastic combination of hot and cold.

RUNNER UP

Viva la Crepe

www.vivelacrepe.fr

51 Spring Street
(between Mulberry & Lafayette Streets)
New York, NY 10012
(855) 273-7369

189 Columbus Avenue
(between 68th & 69th Streets)
New York, NY 10023
(855) 273-7369

1 West 59th Street
(between Fifth & Sixth Avenues)
New York, NY 10019
(855) 273-7369

CRONUT

Dominique Ansel Bakery

www.dominiqueansel.com

189 Spring Street
(between Thompson & Sullivan Streets)
New York, NY 10012
(212) 219-2773

I have been waiting a long time, and after many attempts, I finally got some authentic cronuts. After waking up at 6 am and getting to the bakery at 7 am, I waited an hour until the opening of the bakery. The flavor of the month that I had was peach with bourbon cream and some citrus sugar. The cronut is decently sized, crispy on the outside from being fried and covered in sugar, topped with some icing and filled with cream. Like a croissant, the cronut has numerous layers and like a doughnut it has a nice fry and some delicious flavors. After the first bite, the juiciness of the oil in the doughnut fills your mouth with delicious cream and sweet tasting sugar. The sweetness from the icing and sugar make the cronut delicious. I can clearly see why the cronut is so famous. I don't think I could down more than one of these at a time, but it definitely is a treat.

RUNNER UP

Mille Feuille Baker and Café

www.millefeuille-nyc.com

(Note: Mille Feuille has chocolate cronuts every day.)

552 Laguardia Place
(between Bleecker & 3rd Streets)
New York, NY 10012
(212) 533-4698

CUPCAKES

Sprinkles Cupcakes

www.sprinkles.com

780 Lexington Avenue
(between 60th & 61st Streets)
New York, NY 10065
(212) 207-8375

Sprinkles serves some of the best cupcakes in NYC. My favorites are the milk chocolate cupcake with chocolate cake and chocolate sprinkles and the cinnamon sugar cupcake. The icing on the milk chocolate cupcake is so light, yet so rich, it is amazing. The cinnamon sugar cupcake has a delicious donut-like top with a moist cinnamon cake. Overall, these cupcakes are impeccable.

RUNNER UP

Baked by Melissa

www.bakedbymelissa.com

(212) 842-0220

109 East 42nd Street
(between Lexington & Park Avenues)
New York, NY 10017

2325 Broadway
(between 84th & 85th Streets)
New York, NY 10024

526 Seventh Avenue
(between 38th & 39th Streets)
New York, NY 10018

529 Broadway
(between Spring & Prince Streets)
New York, NY 10012

7 East 14th Street
(between Fifth Avenue & University Place)
New York, NY 10003

Runner Up listings continued on next page...

CUPCAKES

Billy's Bakery

www.billysbakerynyc.com

184 Ninth Avenue
(between West 21st and 22nd Streets)
New York, NY 10011
(212) 647-9956

75 Franklin Street
(between Broadway and Church Street)
New York, NY 10013
(212) 647-9958

1 West 59th Street
(The Plaza Food Hall – Concourse Level)
New York, NY 10019
(212) 371-1133

Buttercup

www.buttercupbakes.nyc

167 Madison Avenue
(at East 33rd Street)
New York, NY 10016
(844) 225-3369

DOUGHNUTS

Doughnut Plant
www.doughnutplant.com

220 West 23rd Street
(between Seventh & Eighth Avenues)
New York, NY 10011
(212) 675-9100

379 Grand Street
(at Norfolk Street)
New York, NY 10002
(212) 505-3700

This is the coolest doughnut place ever with unbelievable flavors and colorful donuts. Depending on the flavor, they come in different sizes and textures. The glazed is perfect – airy, and not too thick. It is sweet and doughy and the flavors of it come together well. The crème brûlée doughnut is small and light with a light cream – my favorite by far. The fresh blueberry is also quite delicious. The square-ish peanut butter and jelly donut is similarly unreal. When you dig in, you feel yourself biting through thick, chunky homemade peanut butter and a layer of fresh jelly. Doughnut Plant is really, really good; like no doughnut place you have ever eaten at before.

RUNNER UP
Dough Brooklyn

www.doughbrooklyn.com

448 Lafayette Avenue
(at Franklin Avenue)
Brooklyn, NY 11205
(347) 533-7544

700 Eighth Avenue
(between 44th & 45th Streets)
New York, NY 10036
(917) 338-1420

14 West 19th Street
(between Fifth & Sixth Avenue)
New York, NY 10011
(212) 243-6844

230 Park Avenue
(Next to Grand Central on 45th Street)
New York, NY 10169
(646) 747-0806

RUNNER UP
Krispy Kreme

www.krispykreme.com

2 Penn Plaza
(inside Penn Station between 31st & 33rd Streets)
New York, NY 10001
(212) 695-0428

DOUGHNUT ICE CREAM SANDWICH

Holey Cream
www.holeycreamnyc.com

796 Ninth Avenue
(between 51st & 52nd Streets)
New York, NY 10019
(212) 247-8400

The delicious doughnut ice cream sandwiches at Holey Cream will make your day. Holey Cream starts with a delicious, hot fresh doughnut (which they slice in half) and then they add rich ice cream in the middle. You are allowed to pick up to three ice cream flavors. There are many ice cream flavors to choose from and some are really creative, but they change often. I like the red velvet cupcake, which is great. I also think their "dulce de leche" ice cream is one of the best flavors I have ever tasted. The ice cream at Holey Cream is so rich and creamy that it is unforgettable. Then you can pick chocolate, strawberry, or vanilla icing to put on top of your donut sandwich and add a topping such as sprinkles or chocolate chips. All together this makes the perfect treat – and the portion is enormous. If you want something really exciting and different – and especially if you can't choose between doughnut and ice cream – this is the perfect dessert or snack.

FROZEN YOGURT

16 Handles
www.16handles.com

153 Second Avenue
(between 9th & 10th Streets)
New York, NY 10003
(212) 260-4414

1569 Second Avenue
(between 81st & 82nd Streets)
New York, NY 10028
(646) 863-2522

325 Amsterdam Avenue
(between 75th & 76th Streets)
New York, NY 10023
(646) 861-1281

178 Eighth Avenue
(at West 19th Street)
New York, NY 10011
(212) 627-2808

428 Third Avenue
(at East 30th Street)
New York, NY 10016
(212) 213-1755

1161 First Avenue
(between East 63rd & 64th Streets)
New York, NY 10065
(646) 707-3424

2600 Broadway
(between West 98th and 99th Streets)
New York, NY 10025
(646) 422-7022

Like its name, 16 Handles, the fun, colorful frozen yogurt shop features 16 handles of different flavored frozen yogurt from which to choose. The flavors change often, but some of my favorites are the thin mint cookies flavor and the cookies and cream. The frozen yogurt is refreshingly cold and creamy. After you are done choosing the right flavor (or flavors) of frozen yogurt, you get to pick from many creative toppings and add them to the top of your yogurt. The toppings consist of fruit, candy, chocolate, and more. Overall, 16 Handles makes great frozen yogurt treats!

GELATO

Amorino
www.amorino.com

60 University Place
(between 10th & 11th Streets)
New York, NY 10003
(212) 253-5599

My favorite gelato in NYC is from Amorino. The Carmello and the chocolate hazelnut are both super smooth and bursting with flavor. The gelato is served in the shape of a flower. There is a nice sweetness and saltiness in the Carmello, while the chocolate hazelnut has a very strong hazelnut flavor. Very amazing gelato!

RUNNER UP

Il Laboratorio del Gelato

www.laboratoriodelgelato.com

188 Ludlow Street
(between Stanton & Houston Streets)
New York, NY 10002
(212) 343-9922

RUNNER UP

M'O Il Gelato

www.mogelato.com

178 Mulberry Street
(between Kenmare & Broome Streets)
New York, NY 10012
(212) 226-6758

52 Gansevoort Street
(between Washington & Greenwich Streets)
New York, NY 10014
(347) 754-2790

GELATO SANDWICH

M'O II Gelato
www.mogelato.com

178 Mulberry Street
(between Kenmare & Broome Streets)
New York, NY 10012
(212) 226-6758

52 Gansevoort Street
(between Washington & Greenwich Streets)
New York, NY 10014
(347) 754-2790

The best and first gelato sandwich I have ever had was at M'O II Gelato. It is one of the best dishes I have ever eaten in my life. I had a bacio (hazelnut) gelato panini which is like an incredibly light circle-shaped, warmed pancake pocket that is filled with the most deliciously creamy hazelnut gelato. The warmness of the buttery light "panini" bread is especially amazing with the contrasting flavor and cold temperature of the gelato.

RUNNER UP

Amorino

www.amorino.com

60 University Place
(between 10th & 11th Streets)
New York, NY 10003
(212) 253-5599

ICE CREAM

Davey's Ice Cream

www.daveysicecream.com

137 First Avenue
(between St. Marks Place & 9th Street)
New York, NY 10003
(212) 228-8032

I have tried many New York City ice creameries and the one that really stands out to me is Davey's Ice Cream. My favorites are the smooth "cookies and cream" and the "speculoos chocolate chip" ice cream. They both stood out as very creamy and delicious — both are jam packed with tons of flavor. The speculoos chocolate chip has chunks of chocolate and speculoos cookie pieces in it and the cookies and cream has soft pieces of Oreo which is key to the texture. I also think the fruity strawberry swirl ice cream is very tasty. Davey's Ice Cream is very memorable and delicious.

RUNNER UP

Emack & Bolio's

www.emackandbolios.com

1564 First Avenue
(between 81st & 82nd Streets)
New York, NY 10028
(212) 734-0105

389 Amsterdam Avenue
(between 78th & 79th Streets)
New York, NY 10024
(212) 362-2747

RUNNER UP

Sundaes and Cones

www.sundaescones.com

95 East 10th Street
(at Third Avenue)
New York, NY 10003
(212) 979-9398

RUNNER UP

Mikey Likes It Ice Cream

www.mikeylikesiticecream.com

199 Avenue A
(between East 12th & 13th Streets)
New York, NY 10009
(646) 896-1836

ICE CREAM CAKE

Parm

www.parmnyc.com

248 Mulberry Street
(between Spring & Prince Streets)
New York, NY 10012
(212) 993-7189

235 Columbus Avenue
(between West 70th & 71st Streets)
New York, NY 10023
(212) 776-4921

250 Vesey Street
(at North End Avenue)
New York, NY 10080
(212) 776-4927

Parm has an array of delicious ice cream cakes. I tried a slice of the classic which was really good. It came with delectable strawberry, chocolate, and pistachio ice cream. It is covered in a cream icing and has some chocolate crispy pieces as the bottom crust. I really enjoyed this ice cream cake and think you will too.

ICE CREAM SANDWICH

Melt Bakery
www.meltbakery.com

132 Orchard Street
(between Rivington & Delancey Streets)
New York, NY 10002
(646) 535-6358

I first tried an ice cream sandwich from a Melt Bakery while walking on the Highline. I had an "Elvis" ice cream sandwich, which was sweet, creamy banana ice cream in between two soft peanut butter cookies. While the sandwich had been frozen in the cart, the cookies were still soft and delicious. The ice cream sandwiches are the perfect size, not too big and not too tiny. I ate the whole thing in less than three minutes. In fact, it was so good I went back to try another flavor. I ended up trying two more that day including the "thick mint" and the red velvet. The Melt Bakery stand sells four separate flavors at a time; these change daily. In addition, the Melt Bakery has an actual store on Orchard Street, where I have tried several other flavors. These ice cream sandwiches are superb – a must try!!!

Coolhaus Ice Cream Sandwiches

www.eatcoolhaus.com

Food Truck
Follow @coolhausNY on Twitter for daily locations
(347) 252-6660

ICE CREAM SUNDAE

Morganstern's

www.morgensternsnyc.com

2 Rivington Street
(between Freeman Alley & Bowery)
New York, NY 10002
(212) 209-7684

The salted caramel pretzel sundae from Morganstern's is perfection. They start with some super moist salted caramel cakes and add three scoops of creamy salted caramel ice cream. Then, they add some salted caramel and thin pretzel pieces. And finally they top it with fresh whipped cream. Super soft. Melty. Salty. Smooth. Delicious.

RUNNER UP

Brooklyn Farmacy and Soda Fountain

www.brooklynfarmacyandsodafountain.com

513 Henry Street
(between Union & Sackett Streets)
Brooklyn, NY 11231
(718) 522-6260

ITALIAN ICES

Lemon Ice King of Corona

www.thelemonicekingofcorona.com

52-02 108th Street
(at Corona Avenue)
Corona, NY 11368
(718) 699-5133

There is a reason this place is legendary. The Lemon Ice King of Corona has the best ices I have ever eaten. The Lemon Ice King of Corona serves a bunch of great flavors (including a terrific lemon), but the one that I crave is the peanut butter ice, which is packed with peanut butter chips. It tastes better than peanut butter, and is so creamy and tasty you won't believe your mouth. Seriously, it is super addictive. Other flavors I especially enjoy are cherry and sour apple. What makes these ices so special is their unique creaminess, with no discernible ice chunks to get in the way. This place is just awesome – and luckily, Is open all year long!

Ralph's Famous Italian Ices

www.ralphsices.com

144 East 24th Street
(between Lexington & Third Avenue)
New York, NY 10010
(212) 533-5333

2361 Hylan Boulevard
Staten Island, NY 10309
(718) 351-8133

3285 Richmond Avenue
Staten Island, NY 10312
(718) 967-1212

4212 Hylan Boulevard
Staten Island, NY 10308
(718) 605-5052

6272 Amboy Road
Staten Island, NY 10309
(718) 605-8133

890 Huguenot Avenue
Staten Island, NY 10312
(718) 356-8133

12-48 Clintonville Street
Whitestone, NY 11357 (Queens)
(718) 746-1456

264-21 Union Turnpike
Floral Park, NY 11004 (Queens)
(718) 343-8724

214-13 41st Avenue
Bayside, NY 11361 (Queens)
(718) 428-4578

MACARONS

Ladurée New York

www.laduree.com

864 Madison Avenue
(between 70th & 71st Streets)
New York, NY 10021
(646) 588-3157

398 West Broadway
(between Broome and Spring Streets)
New York, NY 10012
(646) 392-7868

If you haven't had them, macarons are light, brightly colored sandwich cookies that originated in France. The best macarons are soft, yet flaky with a little bit of crunch in the sandwich cookies, surrounding a kind of light, slightly chewy filling. They come in many flavors such as chocolate, strawberry, pistachio, and salted caramel. Not surprisingly, Ladurée New York (a favorite in Paris) serves up the best macarons in NYC. People are simply addicted to these cookies. It's tough to choose among the many flavors, so unless you have a clear favorite, it's best to mix it up.

RUNNER UP

Macaron Café

www.macaroncafe.com

161 West 36th Street
(between Seventh Avenue & Broadway)
New York, NY 10018
(212) 564-3525

625 Madison Avenue
(at 59th Street)
New York, NY 10022
(212) 486-2470

MOCHI ICE CREAM

Soto
www.sotonyc.com

345 East 12th Street
(between West 4th Street & Washington Place)
New York, NY 10014
(212) 414-3088

I love the mochi at Soto. It comes in multiple flavors such as vanilla, green tea, strawberry, and mango. I like the sweet strawberry the best. The soft casing doesn't have any flour on it which some other places put on their mochi. I usually wait a few minutes before digging into the mochi, because then the ice cream becomes a little melty and not too solid.

RUNNER UP

Beard Papa's

www.beardpapa.com

2167 Broadway
(between 76th & 78th Streets)
New York, NY 10024
(212) 799-3770

RUNNER UP

Sushi Yasuda

www.sushiyasuda.com

204 East 43rd Street
(between Second & Third Avenues)
New York, NY 10017
(212) 972-1001

PIE

Bubby's
www.bubbys.com

120 Hudson Street
(at North Moore Street)
New York, NY 10013
(212) 219-0666

71 Gansevoort Street
(at Washington Street)
New York, NY 10014
(212) 206-6200

Bubby's has the best fresh pies ever in really great flavors such as sour cherry, apple, and key lime. I especially love the sour cherry pie. While they sometimes feature special pies, there is always a variety of pies from which to choose. You can purchase pie by the slice or by the whole pie. Each slice comes with fresh whipped cream, which is a nice touch.

RUNNER UP

Little Pie Company

www.littlepiecompany.com

424 West 43rd Street
(between Ninth & Tenth Avenues)
New York, NY 10036
(212) 736-4780

PLAIN CROISSANT

Petrossian New York Boutique Café

www.petrossian.com/boutique.html

911 Seventh Avenue
(between 57th & 58th Streets)
New York, NY 10019
(212) 245-2217

In preparing this guide, I tasted a lot of croissants, and there is no contest in my book. These are the best in the city. They are soft and flaky, with lots of layers, but at the same time kind of crunchy, yet not too hard. They have a nice buttery taste. When you bite into one of these, it doesn't break apart and keeps its shape. Note that the bakery is separate from the restaurant (which is fancy). The first time I visited, I mistakenly walked into the restaurant and asked if they had croissants to go, but was quickly directed to the adjacent bakery.

RUNNER UP

Ceci Cela

www.cecicelanyc.com

55 Spring Street
(between Lafayette & Mulberry Streets)
New York, NY 10012
(212) 274-9179

POPOVERS

BLT Prime
www.e2hospitality.com/blt-prime

111 East 22nd Street
(between Park & Lexington Avenues)
New York, NY 10010
(212) 995-8500

BLT Prime is definitely my favorite place to get a popover. And I cannot find a popover that is even close to the same caliber as the ones at BLT Prime. You do not have to ask for the popovers — they arrive right after you order and come with sea salt and butter. When you break open the crunchy shell, steam comes out of this incredible gruyere cheese flavored popover. Then, when all the steam goes away, you see the mountains of soft, bready insides. Immediately afterwards, you have to put the butter inside with a little sea salt, close it back up and wait 10 seconds for the butter to melt. Then, and only then, you take your first bite and YUM! There is no match for this popover. They even provide the recipe for these on a little card when they serve them.

POPSICLE

PopBar
www.pop-bar.com

5 Carmine Street
(at Sixth Avenue)
New York, NY 10014
(212) 255-4874

I have been searching for the best popsicle in NYC. My overall favorite place is Popbar on Carmine Street. The popsicles come in many cool (but straightforward) flavors, and are made of either gelato, sorbetto, or yogurt. My favorite popsicle at Popbar is the peanut butter popGelato. It is smooth and creamy and has the perfect sweet peanut butter taste that I love. I also really like their strawberry popSorbetto – which is sweet and refreshing. At Popbar, you can have any of the pops dipped in a topping like milk or dark chocolate, which makes them even tastier. Popbar is a truly delicious and unique shop. If you are craving a great, refreshing dessert, check it out.

RUNNER UP

La NewYorkina Mexican Ice & Sweets

www.lanewyorkina.com

Check their website for cart schedule

RUNNER UP

People's Pops

www.peoplespops.com

(347) 850-2388

(some locations are seasonal – check website or call)

425 West 15th Street
(between Ninth & Tenth Avenues)
New York, NY 10011

118 First Avenue
(between 7th Street & St. Marks Place)
New York, NY 10009

808 Union Street
(at Seventh Avenue)
Brooklyn, NY 11215

PRETZEL

Loreley

www.loreleynyc.com

7 Rivington Street
(between Bowery & Chrystie Streets)
New York, NY 10002
(212) 253-7077

Loreley's pretzels are fresh baked and come in threes. They have an unbelievable aroma. They are dense and crunchy outside, and soft inside. The pretzels are filling, but not huge or oversized, and seem to be made with care. All in all, they are just buttery and amazing. There is a beer garden in the back of the Loreley on Rivington, but they are fine about serving food at the tables in the front of the restaurant. It is definitely worth going to get the pretzels here.

RUNNER UP

Sigmund's Pretzels

www.sigmundnyc.com

29 Avenue B
(between East Second & Third Streets)
New York, NY 10009
(646) 410-0333

SHAVE ICE

Dessert Club, ChikaLicious
www.dessertclubnyc.com

204 East 10th Street
(between First & Second Avenues)
New York, NY 10003
(212) 475-0929

I was very glad that I tried the shave ice at Chickalicious! I went with the Blue Raspberry flavor, but note that it comes in a number of other flavors too like Kiwi Strawberry, Lemon Lime and Green Watermelon. The shave ice is served in a paper cone – it is creamy like a New Orleans snowball, really refreshing and tasty. I was happy to hear that they even serve them all year long, not just in the summer months. The only thing to take note of is that at the center of the ice ball is some kind of dessert cream. The cream tastes good, but in my opinion, there was just too much of it. I ended up leaving about half the cream. All in all though, this is a really fun dessert.

RUNNER UP

Beard Papa's

www.beardpapa.com

2167 Broadway
(between 76th & 77th Streets)
New York, NY 10024
(212) 799-3770

S'MORES

Dominique Ansel Bakery

www.dominiqueansel.com

189 Spring Street
(between Thompson & Sullivan Streets)
New York, NY 10012
(212) 219-2773

The "frozen s'mores" dessert at Dominique Ansel Bakery is special. It consists of a homemade soft marshmallow stuffed with a ball of frozen vanilla custard and surrounded by chocolate covered wafer pieces. It is torched before your eyes and put on a stick. Just an amazing creation that is really, really good.

SOFT SERVE

Momofuku Milk Bar
www.milkbarstore.com

15 West 56th Street
(between Fifth & Sixth Avenues)
New York, NY 10019
(347) 577-9504

382 Metropolitan Avenue
(at Havemeyer)
Brooklyn, NY 11211
(347) 577-9504

251 East 13th Street
(at Second Avenue)
New York, NY 10003
(347) 577-9504

561 Columbus Avenue
(at 87th Street)
New York, NY 10024
(347) 577-9504

360 Smith Street
(at Second Place)
Brooklyn, NY 11231
(347) 577-9504

The cereal milk soft serve ice cream at Momofuku Milk Bar is a delicious treat, and with the addition of crunchy corn flakes, the super cold soft serve is truly amazing.

RUNNER UP

Big Gay Ice Cream
www.biggayicecream.com

125 East 7th Street
(between Avenue A & First Avenue)
New York, NY 10009
(212) 533-9333

61 Grove Street
(between South Seventh Avenue & Sheridan Square)
New York, NY 10014
(212) 414-0222

SORBET

Il Postino
www.ilpostinony.com

337 East 49th Street
(between First & Second Avenues)
New York, NY 10017
(212) 688-0033

If you ever go to Il Postino for a special occasion, save room for dessert because you will not believe your eyes or your taste buds if you order the sorbet, which is the most special sorbet I have ever eaten. The flavors are peach, coconut, pineapple, and lemon. Each flavor sorbet is served in its own corresponding fruit. So the peach comes in a scooped-out frozen peach, and the coconut is served in a small frozen coconut. Each one is positively amazing, but for some reason I like the peach one the very best. The sorbet itself is creamy, refreshing, and bursting with fruity flavor. All in all, a spectacular treat, and the ending to what is always a delicious meal.

STRAWBERRY SHORTCAKE

Veniero's Pasticceria and Caffé

www.venierospastry.com

342 East 11th Street
(between First & Second Avenues)
New York, NY 10003
(212) 674-7070

The strawberry shortcake at Veniero's makes for one extremely tasty snack or dessert. The cake is spongy (in a good way) and perfectly moist, but not soggy. This shortcake contains an awesome homemade light cream that tastes amazing. Inside each cake are layers of a ripe, juicy strawberry filling. The strawberries add a sweet, yet clean flavor to the cake. The milky cream and the sweet strawberry filling balance each other out, which makes the cake just right. Overall, I wouldn't hesitate to make a special trip just to have a slice of this cake – I highly recommend that you give it a try.

RUNNER UP

Lady M. Cake Boutique

www.ladym.com

36 West 40th Street
(between Avenue Of The Americas & Fifth Avenue)
New York, NY 10018
(212) 452-2222

RUNNER UP

Harbs

www.harbsnyc.com

1374 Third Avenue
(at East 78th Street)
New York, NY 10075
(646) 896-1511

198 Ninth Avenue
(at West 22nd Street)
New York, NY 10011
(646) 336-6888

TARTE TATIN

Buvette
www.buvette.com

42 Grove Street
(between Bedford & Bleecker Streets)
New York, NY 10014
(212) 255-3590

The best tarte tatin by far in NYC is the apple tarte tatin from Buvette. It features big slices of caramelized apples in a soft crust. The tart is sweet and soft and gooey and is also unbelievably light. The crust is so light that it breaks apart like a delicate croissant. With a little cream on the side, it is unreal.

Benoit

www.benoitny.com

60 West 55th Street
(between Avenue Of The Americas & Fifth Avenue)
New York, NY 10019
(646) 943-7373

WHOOPIE PIE

Baked
www.bakednyc.com

359 Van Brunt Street
(between Wolcott & Dikeman Streets)
Brooklyn, NY 11231
(718) 222-0345

I set out to find the best whoopie pie in NYC; Baked turned out to be my favorite. Baked has a few flavors, but my favorite is the strawberry whoopie pie. It is sweet, moist strawberry cake that is very soft, with luscious creamy, fresh whipped cream. The whipped cream is extremely light and has the right amount of sweetness so as not to overpower this awesome dessert. (Normally, I really like chocolate whoopie pies as well, but Baked's chocolate pie had an espresso taste that might not appeal to those who don't like the taste of coffee.)

RUNNER UP

Joyce Bakeshop

www.joycebakeshop.com

646 Vanderbilt Avenue
(between Park Place & Prospect Place)
Brooklyn, NY 11238
(718) 623-7470

CHAPTER **6**

BEVERAGES

APPLE TEA

Beyoglu
(no website)

1431 Third Avenue
(at 81st Street)
New York, NY 10028
(212) 650-0850

If you are in the mood for a hot drink that is sweet and also a little sour at the same time, then this is the drink for you. Beyoglu's apple tea is served piping hot. It is perfect for a cold day when you are thirsty – but not too thirsty, as it comes in little glasses with tiny spoons. After you have one, you will want another, trust me. One day I had three of them, and that was before the main course came! The apple tea is so good, it goes with any course and is also delicious with dessert (I always go with the baklava). Also, if you are looking for a cold beverage, the "sour cherry juice" at Beyoglu is thirst-quenching and great.

RUNNER UP

Turkish Kitchen

www.turkishkitchen.com

386 Third Ave
(between 27th & 28th Streets)
New York, NY 10016
(212) 679-6633

CEREAL MILK

Momofuku Milk Bar
www.milkbarstore.com

15 West 56th Street
(between Fifth & Sixth Avenues)
NewYork, NY 10019
(347) 577-9504

251 East 13th Street
(at Second Avenue)
New York, NY 10003
(347) 577-9504

360 Smith Street
(at Second Place)
Brooklyn, NY 11231
(347) 577-9504

382 Metropolitan Avenue
(at Havemeyer)
Brooklyn, NY 11211
(347) 577-9504

561 Columbus Avenue
(at 87th Street)
New York, NY 10024
(347) 577-9504

I love milk and cereal, especially for breakfast. But I have never seen them combined together and served in a milk jug until I went to the Momofuku Milk Bar. I found out that they had their own creation called Cereal Milk™. It is a jug of milk, with the taste of sweet corn flakes (but without any of the mushy, chunky pieces). The sweet flavor that the cornflakes lend to the milk is what makes this unique menu item truly delicious, and a must try!

COOLEST/MOST FUN DRINK

Sugar Factory American Brasserie
www.sugarfactory.com

835 Washington Street
(between 13th & Gansevoort Streets)
New York, NY 10014
(212) 414-8700

The Ocean Blue Goblet is a humongous 60-ounce drink that not only has gummy sharks in it, but also features dry ice. This massive drink comes to your table overflowing with bubbles and smoke from the dry ice. It is super fun to drink this soda-like drink with its sweet, blue raspberry flavor. I like to take out the sharks after they have been soaked in the really cold drink and eat them. Overall, this is a drink you most likely won't find anywhere else.

EGG CREAM

Katz's
www.katzsdelicatessen.com

205 East Houston Street
(at Ludlow Street)
New York, NY 10002
(212) 254-2246

Egg creams are confusingly named. They don't have any egg or any cream in them whatsoever. Instead, their main ingredients are seltzer, milk, and chocolate syrup. That sounds simple, but no two egg creams taste exactly the same. Some taste more like seltzer and others taste more like chocolate (they can also be made with vanilla syrup at some places, but the chocolate egg cream is the classic as far as I am concerned). The egg cream at Katz's Delicatessen is my favorite. It is a little more seltzery than others, and I like that because it is more thirst quenching. They use UBetcha brand chocolate syrup, which tastes really good and works best for egg creams in my opinion. It's everything an egg cream should be. You can't go wrong ordering one here.

RUNNER UP

Eisenberg's Sandwich Shop

www.eisenbergsnyc.com

174 Fifth Avenue
(between 22nd & 23rd Streets)
New York, NY 10010
(212) 675-5096

RUNNER UP

Lexington Candy Shop

www.lexingtoncandyshop.net

1226 Lexington Avenue
(at 83rd Street)
New York, NY 10028
(212) 288-0057

FROZEN HOT CHOCOLATE

Serendipity 3
www.serendipity3.com

225 East 60th Street
(between Second & Third Avenues)
New York, NY 10022

Serendipity is famous for their astounding frozen hot chocolate. It is ice cold and refreshing, while still having the delicious flavor of a rich hot chocolate. Topped with milk chocolate shavings and a ridiculous amount of whipped cream, the frozen hot chocolate at Serendipity is a unique creation and a must try.

HOT CHOCOLATE

L.A. Burdick Chocolate Shop and Café
www.burdickchocolate.com

5 East 20th Street
(between Broadway & Fifth Avenue)
New York, NY 10003
(212) 796-0143

The milk chocolate hot chocolate at L.A. Burdick is my favorite in NYC. It is extremely rich and creamy hot chocolate that is pleasantly thick. They give you the hot chocolate right after they make it, so it is piping hot. This hot chocolate is very special and delicious – it simply cannot be beaten.

Max Brenner

www.maxbrenner.com

841 Broadway
(between 13th & 14th Streets)
New York, NY 10003
(212) 388-0030

MILKSHAKES

Big Daddy's
www.bigdaddysnyc.com

239 Park Avenue South
(between 19th & 20th Streets)
New York, NY 10003
(212) 477-1500

1596 Second Avenue
(between 82nd & 83rd Streets)
New York, NY 10028
(212) 717-2020

2454 Broadway
(between 90th & 91st Streets)
New York, NY 10024
(212) 677-2004

Big Daddy's is making some of the best milkshakes in NYC. After going there and trying many of the various milkshakes, my favorite is the "Bananas Foster" milkshake, which consists of sweet caramel, vanilla ice cream and bananas. The milkshake is super cold, thick and simply incredible. I also like the "Cotton Candy Circus Shake" milkshake which is served with a mound of cotton candy on top. Big Daddy's is a find with some of the coolest and tastiest milkshake flavors around.

RUNNER UP

Island Burgers and Shakes

www.islandburgersandshakes.com

422 Amsterdam Avenue
(at 80th Street)
New York, NY 10024
(212) 877-7934

766 Ninth Avenue
(between 51st & 52nd Streets)
New York, NY 10019
(212) 307-7934

Runner Up listings continued on next page...

MILKSHAKES

Schnipper's Quality Kitchen

www.schnippers.com

23 East 23rd Street

(between Park & Madison Avenues)
New York, NY 10010
(212) 233-1025

620 Eighth Avenue

(at 41st Street)
New York, NY 10018
(212) 921-2400

SLUSHIES

Dylan's Candy Bar

www.dylanscandybar.com

1011 Third Avenue
(between 60th & 61st Streets)
New York, NY 10021
(646) 735-0078

The Café at Dylan's Candy Bar has very good, ice cold slushies that are made in a genuine slushy machine. They have the classic blue raspberry and cherry flavors. It's much harder to find a good slushy in NYC than it should be, so when you are craving a cold slushy, definitely give Dylan's Candy Bar a try.

7 Eleven

www.7-eleven.com

Numerous locations throughout NYC

SMOOTHIES

Jamba Juice
www.jambajuice.com

Numerous locations throughout NYC

Jamba Juice is all about serving up the perfect smoothies: it offers some food items like flatbreads and some other baked goods, but unlike other places that offer smoothies on the side, the focus at Jamba Juice is definitely the smoothies. My favorite smoothie at Jamba Juice is called the Razzmatazz. It is a mixture of mixed berry juice, strawberries, bananas, and orange sherbet. It is served very cold and is very refreshing. It has a hint of sourness from the orange sherbet, but is not so sour that it puckers your mouth. Jamba Juice also has many other delicious smoothies such as the mango-a-go-go (mango-based), strawberries wild (strawberry-banana based), and banana berry (bananas with blueberry, apple-strawberry, and raspberry flavors).

CONCLUSION

So there you have it — my favorite places to eat and drink in New York City — at least as of the date of this publication. But, as everyone knows, the restaurant scene in New York is ever-changing. Restaurants come and go, and I'm always discovering new favorites. In fact, while working on this book, I had to make several changes to include new favorites and, sadly, to delete some favorites from places that closed their doors. At the end of the day, I made every effort to provide you with the most current information: the info is as up-to-date as possible.

With that said, I hope that you will help be my eyes and ears on the streets of New York. If you find a restaurant that you think bears consideration for inclusion in the next edition, please let me know. I always enjoy trying out new places — research is a tough job, but I am happy to do research when it comes to food.

You can contact me through my website www.pinespicks.com or send me an email at suggestions@pinespicks.com. I'll be posting reviews and additional write-ups there from time to time so I can continue to provide the most updated info regarding the best places to eat and drink in New York City.

David Pines

INDEX

Note: Bold page numbers indicate a "Pines Pick" choice

L

L&B Spumoni Gardens, **39**
La Bonne Soupe, 50
L.A. Burdick Chocolate Shop and
    Café, 93, **130**
La Nacional, 64
La NewYorkina Mexican Ice &
    Sweets, 116
La Paella, **64**
La Pain Quotidien, **80**
Ladurée New York, **111**
Lady M. Cake Boutique, 122
Lemon Ice King of Corona, **110**
Levain Bakery, 92, 95
Lexington Candy Shop, 129
Little Muenster, 24
Little Pie Company, 113
lobster
    macaroni and cheese, 45
    rolls, 75
lollipop wings, 16
Lombardi's, **38**
Lorley, **117**
Lucky's Famous Burgers, 31
Luke's Lobster, **78**
Luzzo's, 38

M

Macaron Café, 111
macaroni and cheese, 28-29
    buffalo chicken macaroni
        and cheese, 28
    lobster macaroni and
        cheese, 45
macarons, 111
MacBar, 29
M'O Il Gelato, 104, **105**
madelines, 93
Magnolia Bakery, **80**
Maison Kayser, **83**
Mamoun's Falafel Restaurant, 54
Mark Restaurant, The, 8
Mary's Fish Camp, **75**
Max Brenner, 29, **89**, **90**, 130
Mediterranean spreads, 59
Melt Bakery, **108**
Melt Shop, The, 24
Mikey Likes It Ice Cream, 106
milk and cookie shots, 94
milkshakes, 131-132
Mille Feuille Baker and Café, 98

milos special, 56
mochi ice cream, 112
Momofuku Milk Bar, **120**, **127**
Morganstern's, **109**
most fun drink, 128
mozzarella sticks, 30
Murray's Cheese Shop, **24**
Murray's Melt, The, 24
mussels, 76

N

nachos, 60
Naruto Ramen, 67
New England clam chowder, 77
New York Burder Co., 43
99 Miles To Philly, 20
noodles, 61
Norma's, **5**, **10**
Northern Tiger, **66**
Num Pang, **41**

O

ocean blue goblets, 128
Oceana, 74
onion rings, 31
"oreo" style cookies, 94
Our Place China Chalet, **57**, **66**

P

pad thai, 63
paella, 64
Palm, The, **87**
pancakes, 11
Parm, **107**
pasta
    baked ziti, 32
    capellini, 32
    macaroni and cheese, 28-29
    plain ziti and sauce, 33
    spaghetti and meatballs, 33
Pastrami Queen, **34**
pastrami sandwiches, 34
Paticceria Rocco, 85
Patricia's, **57**
Patsy's Italian Restaurant, **33**
peanut butter
    ice cream, 35
    Italian ices, 110
    peanut butter and jelly
        sandwiches, 35
    popGelatos, 116
Peanut Butter & Co., **35**

Pearl Oyster Bar, **77**
Peking duck sliders, 62
People's Pops, 116
Peter Luger Steak House, 45
Petitle Abeille, 13
Petrossian New York Boutique
    Café, **114**
Phillipe Chow, **52**
pierogis, 65
pies, 113
    whoopie pies, 124
Pietro's, **42**
Pines Picks, 1
Pink Teacup, **11**
pizza
    bayou beast, 40
    chocolate, 89
    flatbread, 36
    regular NYC slice, 37
    sicilian square, 39
    thin crust/brick oven, 38
    unique slice, 40
plain ziti and sauce, 33
Plenty Café, **94**
Pluck U, **30**
Polo Bar, The, **18**
polo burgers, 18
PopBar, **116**
Popeyes, 21
popovers, 115
popsicles, 116
pork
    buns, 66
    pork and chive dumplings,
        66
    ribs, 42
    sandwiches, 41
potatoes
    gnocci, 57
    knish, 58
pretzels, 117
provencale mussels, 76
pudding, banana, 80
pulled pork sandwiches, 41

R

rainbow bagels, 4
Ralph's Famous Italian Ices, 110
ramen, 67
Ranch1, **44**
Rare Bar and Grill, **16**
razzmatazz, 134

ABOUT DAVID PINES

Born and raised (so far) in New York City, tenth grader David Pines loves to surf – restaurant guides, that is. But he never found a guide or website that captured all the best spots for kids. That's when David decided to create his own guide to the ever-exciting and ever-changing New York restaurant scene. Along with various members of his family, David went on food hunts throughout the City to find the very best dishes for kids. The result was the First Edition of *Pines Picks, A Kid's Guide to the Best Things to Eat and Drink in New York City* published when he was in the sixth grade, and the Second Edition published when he was in the eighth grade. David has been interviewed by newspapers, magazines and bloggers from across the US, Europe, and Australia. Since that time, David has continued to explore the dizzying array of offerings from the thousands of NYC eateries. He has also attempted to track the openings and closings of so many NYC spots. Sadly, some of the restaurants that closed were among his favorites. This Third Edition of Pines Picks reflects all of David's latest findings.

In addition to participating in food hunts, David burns thousands of calories a week playing competitive tennis. He is also an avid skier who can find the best lunch spots at any mountain resort. David loves to travel – especially when it means getting an opportunity to try all the local cuisine.

Made in the USA
Columbia, SC
16 December 2022

74245468R00083